W9-BLP-327

HEALTH REPORTS:
DISEASES AND DISORDERS

ALTERNATIVE MEDICINE

CATHERINE G. DAVIS

TWENTY-FIRST CENTURY BOOKS
MINNEAPOLIS

Cover image: Using natural ingredients such as herbs to fight medical ailments is just one form of alternative medicine.

USA TODAY®, its logo, and associated graphics are federally registered trademarks. All rights are reserved. All USA TODAY text, graphics, and photographs are used pursuant to a license and may not be reproduced, distributed, or otherwise used without the express written consent of Gannett Co., Inc.

USA TODAY Snapshots®, graphics, and excerpts from USA TODAY articles on pages 6–7, 14–15, 18, 21, 30–31, 35, 36–37, 46–47, 50–51, 56, 62–63, 67, 68–69, 76, 78–79, 84–85, 94–95, 97, and 98–99 © copyright 2012 by USA TODAY.

Twenty-First Century Books
A division of Lerner Publishing Group, Inc.
241 First Avenue North
Minneapolis, MN 55401 U.S.A.

Website address: www.lernerbooks.com

Library of Congress Cataloging-in-Publication Data

Davis, Catherine G.
    Alternative medicine / by Catherine G. Davis.
        p.   cm. — (USA Today health reports: diseases and disorders)
    Includes bibliographical references and index.
    ISBN 978-0-7613-8145-7 (lib. bdg. : alk. paper)
    1. Alternative medicine—Juvenile literature. I. Title.
 R733.B555 2012
 616—dc23   2011025441

Manufactured in the United States of America
1 – DP – 12/31/11

CONTENTS

USA TODAY
HEALTH REPORTS:
DISEASES AND DISORDERS

TAKING A BROAD APPROACH TO HEALTH

ALICE'S STORY

Alice had been healthy all her life. She had never broken any bones or had any surgeries. Then, just before her thirty-fifth birthday, she was diagnosed with a brain tumor. After meeting with her family doctor, she was referred to a brain surgeon who specialized in the type of tumor Alice had. He was confident that Alice's tumor was not cancerous. But it was in a dangerous location. If allowed to grow, the tumor would make it impossible for Alice to breathe or swallow on her own. Her heart would not beat on its own either. The surgeon recommended surgery to remove the tumor.

After discussing the situation with her family, Alice agreed to move ahead with the surgery. After the twelve-hour procedure, the lab confirmed that the tumor was not cancerous. Alice stayed in the hospital for a week before her doctors released her to recover at home. Physically, Alice's healing went very well, and her medical team was very pleased with the outcome of the surgery. But Alice had been suffering from depression and anxiety ever since her diagnosis. In talking with her family doctor, Alice decided to take a complementary approach to her emotional health. She would fill the prescription from her doctor for an antianxiety-antidepressant medication. And she would also give an alternative therapy—acupuncture—a try. Alice found great relief from acupuncture. It helped calm and relax her, and she felt better after each session. In fact, Alice has incorporated acupuncture as a part of managing her overall health.

Alternative medicine is a loose term for a type of health care that relies on practices and traditions outside of conventional medicine.

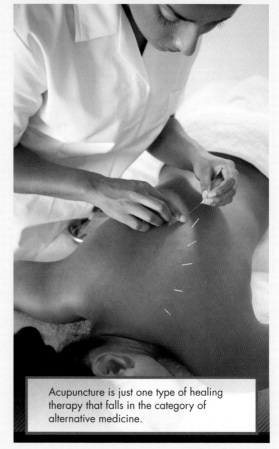

Conventional medicine is based on the idea that diseases cause people to become ill. Illnesses are treated with drugs, surgery, or both. Used in place of conventional medicine, alternative medicine aims to relieve pain and stress, recover from illness or injury, and to stay healthy. Alternative medicine may include herbal treatments, aromatherapy, and a carefully controlled diet, for example.

Acupuncture is just one type of healing therapy that falls in the category of alternative medicine.

Alternative medicine has also come to be known as *complementary* or *integrative* medicine. It includes a range of healing practices that patients use along with conventional medicine for the same reasons. These types of practices offer healing therapies such as acupuncture, hypnosis, chiropractic massage, and other techniques of promoting good health. Many Americans rely on integrative medicine to manage their health.

Over the years, physicians have increasingly come to accept and recommend integrative practices for their patients. In addition, insurance companies have begun to pay for acupuncture treatments, chiropractic sessions, and other methods that help patients deal with pain.

In this book, the term *alternative medicine* is used to refer to the

April 1, 2009

From the Pages of USA TODAY

Yoga gets a room to breathe

NEW YORK—Fashion is the last thing on Donna Karan's mind at the moment. When she says the designer's role is "not only to dress people but to address them as well," it is clear she will not be chatting about her latest wardrobe creations.

A longtime practitioner of yoga and meditation, she has contributed $850,000 to the Beth Israel Medical Center to bring yoga therapy and a new kind of caregiving to the cancer wing. Sitting in her Urban Zen studio on Greenwich Street and sipping a bottle of green vegetable and fruit juice, Karan launches into a personal monologue about how she hopes to make a difference.

[The] total person, she says, needs both the science from the Western world and healing and alternative medicines from the Eastern culture. The latter was absent when her husband died from lung cancer in 2001 and her best friend [died from] brain cancer last September. Her grant to Beth Israel, called the Urban Zen Initiative, provides cancer patients another caregiver to stand alongside the doctors and nurses.

High hopes for the research

Called "integrative therapists," they teach easy yoga poses and breathing techniques, most of which are done in bed and are designed to help ease patient discomfort from surgeries, treatments and anxiety. They also offer patients meditative tapes during treatments, help them access all levels of care and reach out to family members.

Karan believes the research attached to the one-year grant will show that hospital

wide range of traditions that are available for managing health. They may be practiced in combination with conventional medicine or as replacements. Readers should keep in mind that it is best to consult with a trained medical professional such as a family physician before trying any type of integrative medicine. Some practices are not supported by scientific research and may, in fact, be dangerous. None of the information in this book is meant as advice for a specific stays can be shortened and fewer anxiety drugs administered, which would save the patient and insurance companies money.

"If this is something we're going to go out and convince hospitals around the country to replicate, we have to be able to show it saves money in the long run or at least is cost-neutral and you end up with happier patients," says Benjamin Killer, director of the research.

Not everyone sees a need

But there are skeptics. David Gorski, an oncologist [tumor specialist] and associate professor at Wayne State University School of Medicine in Detroit [MI], does not see a need for integrative therapists and does not believe many hospitals could hire them, anyway.

"If an 'alternative' medical treatment is found by science to be useful, physicians will happily integrate it into scientific medicine, and it will then be just 'medicine,' " Gorski says.

Karan disagrees. "The nurses and doctors are too busy. We need to think outside the box and find ways to effectively change the medical system."

Fashion designer Donna Karan donated money to Beth Israel Medical Center in New York City for yoga therapy and other caregiving for cancer patients.

When her friend and former model Lynn Kohlman was diagnosed with breast cancer, Karan introduced her to yoga. Kohlman practiced regularly with Karan, even after she developed brain cancer and was given four months to live. She lived 5 1/2 years.

"After the brain surgery, the doctors said they had never found someone who had been able to be so calm. She found her inner strength," Karan says.

—Janice Lloyd

medical problem. The goal of this book is to help you become a wise consumer of the growing field of alternative medicine.

Thousands of alternative treatment approaches are possible. While this book does not attempt to address them all, it includes discussions of many popular kinds of alternative therapies. Included are hypothetical cases that represent situations in which alternative-medicine techniques might be considered.

CHAPTER ONE

WHAT IS ALTERNATIVE MEDICINE?

ANDY'S STORY

For weeks Andy hadn't been feeling right. During a getaway visit to his beach house, he noticed a vague sensation of bloating in his abdomen. By the time he returned to work on Monday, his stomach hurt. Andy's job as a lawyer had been stressful in recent months. At first, he thought he might have a touch of indigestion from working late and not eating right. But Andy vomited after dinner twice the following week. Soon after he noticed he was losing weight.

Andy went to his family doctor for a series of tests. They confirmed the doctor's suspicions: Andy had a peptic ulcer—a break in the lining of the digestive tract. He also had gastritis—an inflammation of the stomach lining. Any number of things can cause these health problems or make them worse, including bacteria, stress, and poor diet.

Andy's doctor recommended that he take a prescription drug to cut down on the amount of acid his stomach was producing. That, in turn, would allow the ulcer to heal. Andy's doctor also recommended an antibiotic to kill any bacteria that may have been responsible for the ulcer. Finally, the doctor suggested that Andy begin a fiber-rich, low-acid diet. The doctor also said that Andy could consider taking a prescription tranquilizer to help manage his work-related stress.

Andy knew that his ulcer was serious enough to require medical attention. But before he took his doctor's advice, he decided to check out another option. He had heard about a trend in health care called alternative, or integrative, medicine. This approach to illness uses a variety of natural remedies such as herbs, relaxation techniques, and acupuncture to bring about healing. Never a fan of prescription drugs, Andy decided to consult his friend Maria. She is a specialist *in alternative medicine, and Andy wanted to get her advice on his situation.*

Maria is a doctor trained in naturopathy, or natural medicine. She is also a licensed acupuncturist. Maria reviewed Andy's test results and had a long talk with him about his lifestyle, diet, work, and personal background. As a naturopath, Maria believes that the body has the power to heal itself. She believes that the body's natural state is one of physical and mental equilibrium, or balance. When that balance is disrupted, as it was in Andy's case, it is important to find out the underlying causes. That is what Maria was trying to discover.

After learning more about Andy, Maria recommended a combination of alternative therapies. Her advice was designed to reduce the acidity in Andy's digestive tract. Her plan would also help heal the digestive tissue and reduce the stress that Andy was feeling.

The first step was for Maria to make sure that Andy did not have high blood pressure. He didn't, so Maria recommended a powder made from slippery elm, an herb native to North America. The slippery elm, she suggested, might help to reduce acidity and soothe the mucous membranes of Andy's stomach and intestines.

In addition, Maria told Andy that he could benefit from acupuncture treatments. In this ancient Chinese practice, the acupuncturist inserts fine, sharp needles into certain key spots on the skin. This produces favorable neural (brain) and chemical responses in the body. Acupuncture is often used to relieve pain and stress. Maria felt it would also help reduce the amount of acid that Andy's stomach was producing.

Maria also recommended that Andy begin eating a fiber-rich diet. She told him to focus on eating small, frequent meals to help reduce bloating and stomach pain. Finally, she suggested that Andy consider hypnosis therapy. Hypnosis can help people change unhealthy behavior patterns as part of changing stressful lifestyles like Andy's.

Consulting with your medical doctor about any alternative treatments you plan to pursue is important.

Andy didn't make a decision right away about which course of therapy to go with. He went home and thought things over carefully. A few days later, he consulted with his regular medical doctor about the steps Maria had suggested. Once he felt he had all the information before him, he made his choice: He would start the fiber-rich diet recommended by both his regular doctor and Maria. He would take the antibiotic to eliminate any harmful bacteria in his system. Andy also agreed to try the herbal remedies that Maria had recommended to help heal his digestive system. He also would consider hypnotherapy to help him manage the stress in his life. Andy said no to prescription tranquilizers and decided to wait before trying acupuncture.

Most important, Andy made sure that both his regular doctor and Maria knew the details of all the treatments he was following. Andy took this important step to avoid complications and unhealthy physical reactions to his treatments.

In a few weeks, Andy was feeling better. A year after his bout with a peptic ulcer, the problem had not come back.

Before hospitals, physicians, test tubes, and pharmacies, people turned to nature and folk traditions to stay healthy and to cure sickness. Native American and Eastern healers used herbs, shrubs, and tree bark to mend wounds, stop pain, and ward off disease. About three thousand years ago, the Chinese began practicing acupuncture. In addition, shamans, or medicine men, throughout Asia, Africa, and the Americas diagnosed illness by observing the way a person looked and acted. These healers noted the color of a person's tongue, the pace of the heartbeat, the person's mood, and dream patterns, among other things, to figure out what was wrong.

In the modern world of gene therapy and fast-paced trauma centers, these techniques may not be the first ones you think of to deal with illness. But the health practices of ancient civilizations are still with us in the twenty-first century. In fact, millions of people around the world continue to rely on herbal medicine, acupuncture, and other ancient remedies as their main form of health care.

In recent years, about 75 percent of Americans have tried some form of alternative medicine to supplement—or in some cases to replace—conventional modern medicine. Some of these people are turning to debated treatments, such as nutrition therapy or magnetic-field therapy, to treat deadly illnesses. These treatments are not scientifically proven to be effective. Family and other mainstream doctors typically do not prescribe them.

Treatments such as these have come to be known as alternative medicine. Generally speaking, scientific studies have not proven that these therapies are effective. Or studies may not have been conducted in enough depth to prove whether or not the alternative treatments are safe and effective. For these reasons, most conventional, or Western, medical doctors (MDs) do not routinely prescribe them, nor do individuals such as physical therapists, psychologists, and registered nurses, who also provide health-care services to patients.

CAM

Complementary/integrative medicine is often called CAM for "complementary and alternative medicine." In CAM, alternative and conventional treatments are prescribed. Integrative medicine treats the whole person—body, mind, and spirit—rather than only individual physical symptoms of a disease or disorder. People who practice alternative medicine also focus on prevention of disease as a key goal.

The categories of alternative medicine include these:

- **Herbs and other dietary supplements.** These supplements include plant-based products, vitamins, and minerals sold over the counter (without a prescription). This category also includes aromatherapy. This therapy involves the use of fragrances made from plant-based materials to create relaxing sensations. It also can help with physical and mental healing.

Herbal remedies and dietary supplements can be bought at many stores. They do not require a prescription from a doctor.

Yoga is a popular practice for many in the United States. The series of movements can positively impact physical and mental health.

- **Mind-body health.** This practice focuses on the interactions among the brain, mind, body, and behavior. It looks at the way these interactions influence physical health. Treatments include meditation, yoga, deep-breathing exercises, tai chi, and music therapy.
- **Hands-on treatments.** These treatments focus on the bones, joints, tissues, muscles, and circulatory and lymphatic systems. Treatments include spinal manipulation as well as chiropractic and massage therapy.
- **Energy-based therapy.** This therapy is based on the belief that imbalances in the body's energy lead to illness. Balance is restored through a variety of practices such as acupuncture, qigong, and Reiki.

Life
SECTION D
LIFE.USATODAY.COM

October 13, 2004

From the Pages of USA TODAY

Power of a super attitude; Reeve's life bolsters theories on mind-body health link

The connection between attitude and well-being has long been suspected, but in recent years scientists studying the mind-body connection are finding that an optimistic outlook can improve more than just mental health.

Christopher Reeve [the star of several Superman movies], who was paralyzed in a horseback riding accident nine years ago and died this week, is to some researchers an example of just how a positive attitude can contribute to an improved physical state.

"There is no doubt in my mind his positive attitude extended his life—probably dramatically. The fact that it didn't allow him to recover function of all limbs is beside the point," says Carol Ryff, a psychology professor at the University of Wisconsin-Madison who has been studying whether high levels of psychological well-being benefit physical health.

"There is a science that is emerging that says a positive attitude isn't just a state of mind," she says. "It also has linkages to what's going on in the brain and in the body."

Ryff has shown that people with higher levels of well-being have lower cardiovascular risk, lower levels of stress hormones and lower levels of inflammation, which serves as a marker of the immune system.

Her research on positive mental states is among 44 grants for the evaluation of optimism that are being financed by the National Institutes of Health. Most research in this area has focused on negative feelings, such as how stress, anxiety and depression affect physical health.

Hard to measure happiness

It's clear that stressors produce abnormal changes in the immune system, says Ronald Glaser, director of Ohio State University's Institute for Behavioral

Medicine Research. Glaser and his wife, Janice Kiecolt-Glaser, a clinical psychologist also at Ohio State, studied the mind-body connection and found that chronic stress and psychological stress can [stop] wounds from healing, might [lessen] the effectiveness of vaccines and can weaken the immune system of caregivers.

Kiecolt-Glaser says there is less definitive work on the benefits of a positive outlook because clearly defined scales, such as those used to measure depression, don't exist for studying happiness.

That makes a positive attitude much more difficult to quantify.

"In laboratories, there are lots of easy ways to make people depressed or anxious for a long period of time. It's harder to make people happy," Kiecolt-Glaser says. "The whole distress, anxiety, depression part matters more, from everything we know, than positive emotions. It's not as easy to see a positive effect."

"Mind-body medicine is now scientifically proven," says Herbert Benson, a cardiologist and associate professor of medicine at Harvard Medical School who is considered a pioneer in the field. "There are literally thousands of articles on how the mind and brain affect the body."

"When a person can focus on something other than illness, it allows the body to take advantage of our own healing capacity," Benson says. "Hope in something beyond the illness, and dedicating oneself to cures for the illness" rather than dwelling on one's illness "gives purpose to life" and helps prevent the negative effects of stress while medical science does its work.

Feel-good alternatives

Medical science also is taking note of alternative medicine. Craig Hospital in Englewood, Colo., has worked with the Reeve Paralysis Foundation to benefit people with spinal cord injuries. Terry Chase, the hospital's coordinator of patient and family education, has been confined to a wheelchair since being hit by a drunken driver while riding her bicycle 16 years ago. She says the hospital's alternative-medicine program provides acupuncture, massage and aromatherapy to help patients feel better and stay positive.

She says the staff does "whatever we can to put people in a better place for their own healing—whatever healing they're going to have. We can't say it will cure them, but it may help them feel better and be more relaxed."

Perhaps one of the most vocal advocates for the power of a positive attitude is Bernie Siegel, a surgeon, author and motivational speaker known for such books as *Love, Medicine & Miracles* and *Peace, Love & Healing*.

"When people are willing to make an effort to cure what's incurable, I'll work with them," he says. "What goes on in your head affects your body."

—*Sharon Jayson*

- **Whole medical systems.** These systems have developed over time in many cultures, separately from conventional medicine. Whole medical systems that evolved in Eastern cultures include Ayurvedic medicine (from India) and traditional Chinese medicine. Western whole medical practices include homeopathy and naturopathy. Native American traditional medicine is also included in this group.

Topping the list of alternative practices to which many Americans turn are relaxation techniques (such as meditation and yoga) and chiropractic medicine. Other popular treatments include spiritual healing, herbal medicine, and hypnosis.

NCCAM

The U.S. National Institutes of Health started the Office of Alternative Medicine in 1991. It was renamed the National Center for Complementary and Alternative Medicine (NCCAM) in 1998. The mission of NCCAM is to "define, through rigorous scientific investigation, the usefulness and safety of complementary and alternative medicine interventions and their roles in improving health and health care."

Many alternative therapies and practitioners have not undergone the strict research and training required for conventional therapies. As with any medical treatment, risks are associated with alternative medicine. The NCCAM suggests that people select practitioners carefully, researching their training and experience. Individuals also must be aware of any side effects of dietary supplements. Patients should know that dietary supplements can sometimes cause problems when taken along with synthetic medications. Above all, it is very important for individuals to tell their doctors about any alternative treatments they are using.

CONVENTIONAL MEDICINE

Conventional medicine relies on a disease model of health, in which diseases are thought to be the cause of human illness. This model of health is largely rooted in science-based research and technology (as are many CAM treatments). It is known as Western medicine because it was developed over many centuries, mainly in the Western Hemisphere—chiefly Europe and the United States. In the United States, the U.S. government strictly regulates conventional medicine. Drugs and clinical procedures undergo rigorous scientific testing. Medical doctors go through years of academic and clinical training before they can legally treat patients.

Many doctors of conventional medicine specialize in specific parts of the body or specific diseases. Examples include cardiologists (heart specialists), oncologists (tumor specialists), and psychologists (mental health specialists). Most doctors focus on diagnosing and treating the symptoms of people who are already ill. These doctors use synthetic medications, surgery, and sophisticated machines to treat diseases and bring about healing.

In contrast, alternative medicine does not rely on surgery, sophisticated technology, or prescription drugs. Instead, it uses herbs, natural oils, massage, and spiritual methods, among other techniques, to treat symptoms and encourage general well-being.

While most conventional doctors focus mainly on treating existing illnesses, alternative medicine puts equal emphasis on maintaining good health. All medical practitioners—both conventional and alternative—agree that good health starts with a few key elements. These elements include the following:

- Eating a healthy, well balanced diet
- Exercising regularly
- Quitting smoking
- Avoiding stress and/or learning to manage stress

In recent years, students in U.S. medical schools have begun studying herbal remedies, acupuncture, and other alternative treatments. They use strict scientific methods to evaluate the safety and effectiveness of these practices. Some medical schools are also teaching certain alternative techniques to students studying to be doctors.

Experts in mainstream Western medicine have accepted some alternative treatments as safe and useful when practiced responsibly. For example, medical researchers have found that acupuncture is an effective therapy for pain and nausea associated with certain medical conditions. And physicians often recommend vitamin supplements, massage therapy, or relaxation techniques such as yoga to their patients. But many physicians and medical researchers remain highly skeptical of alternative therapies. They worry that people will bypass conventional medicine and choose unproven treatments, putting their health—and even their lives—at risk.

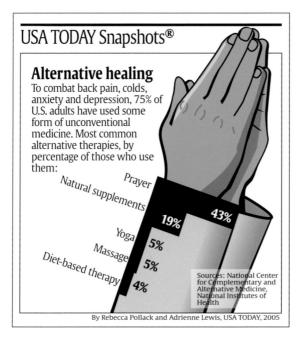

USA TODAY Snapshots®

Alternative healing

To combat back pain, colds, anxiety and depression, 75% of U.S. adults have used some form of unconventional medicine. Most common alternative therapies, by percentage of those who use them:

Natural supplements — Prayer

Prayer 43%

Natural supplements 19%

Yoga 5%

Massage 5%

Diet-based therapy 4%

Sources: National Center for Complementary and Alternative Medicine, National Institutes of Health

By Rebecca Pollack and Adrienne Lewis, USA TODAY, 2005

WHO USES ALTERNATIVE MEDICINE?

A survey by the National Center for Health Statistics and NCCAM in the early 2000s found that in the United States about 75 percent of adults have used some form of alternative medicine.

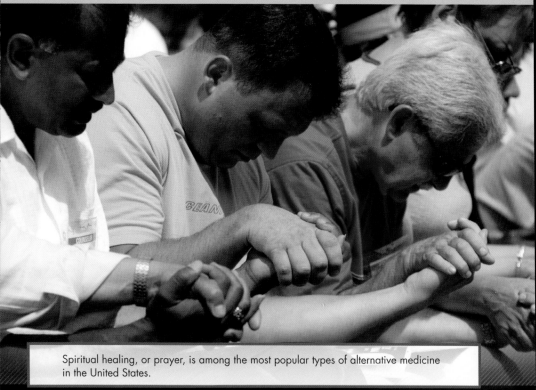

Spiritual healing, or prayer, is among the most popular types of alternative medicine in the United States.

More women than men use it. The most popular therapies are spiritual healing (prayer), followed by the use of herbs, deep breathing and meditation, chiropractic medicine, and yoga. People turn to alternative medicine to address many complaints. The most common is back pain, followed by pain in joints, anxiety, high cholesterol, and the common cold.

GOVERNMENT REGULATION AND INSURANCE COVERAGE

Since the early 1990s, the U.S. government has tried to protect citizens against harmful substances and fraudulent claims. The U.S. Food and Drug Administration (FDA) monitors the safety of dietary supplements once they are available for sale to consumers.

The Federal Trade Commission (FTC) oversees advertising. No national system for the licensing of practitioners of alternative

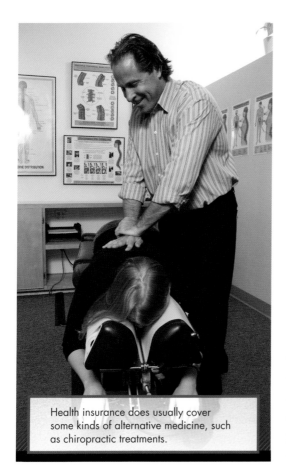

Health insurance does usually cover some kinds of alternative medicine, such as chiropractic treatments.

treatments exists as there does for medical doctors. Some professionals, such as chiropractors, are licensed in all states. However, the specific requirements for training and testing vary from state to state. Other practices (such as Reiki and acupuncture) may not require licenses at all. When choosing a practitioner, it is smart to consult with your medical doctor first. You can also check with professional organizations that specialize in certain types of treatment. For example, the American Association of Naturopathic Physicians can tell you whether your state has formal requirements for people who practice naturopathic medicine and what those requirements are. The American Chiropractic Association can give the same kind of information about chiropractors in your state.

Health insurance programs usually cover certain types of alternative therapies. The most common are acupuncture and chiropractic treatments. Insurance companies usually limit the number of treatments they will pay for each year. This means that some of the cost of this type of treatment is paid by the individual. So

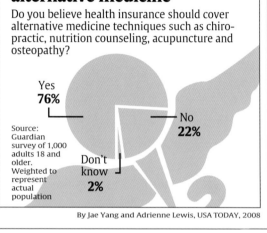

USA TODAY Snapshots®

Health insurance and alternative medicine

Do you believe health insurance should cover alternative medicine techniques such as chiropractic, nutrition counseling, acupuncture and osteopathy?

Yes
76%

No
22%

Don't know
2%

Source: Guardian survey of 1,000 adults 18 and older. Weighted to represent actual population

By Jae Yang and Adrienne Lewis, USA TODAY, 2008

before you make an appointment for any type of alternative treatment, be sure to research your insurance plan.

And always remember to tell all of your health-care providers about any alternative treatment you are considering. All your health-care professionals have a common goal—to work with you to help you make healthier lifestyle choices and to achieve and maintain a healthy mind and body. As Dr. Paul Limburg of the Mayo Clinic points out, "If you spend most of your day lying on the couch and eating potato chips, taking a supplement to help you lose weight or practicing techniques to boost your immune system likely isn't going to do you much good."

Of course, any medical product or procedure—conventional or alternative—can be risky. The practice of any kind of medicine is not an exact science—even conventional medicine. There is never a 100 percent guarantee that treatment will work in every case. The best way to evaluate the promises and risks of alternative and conventional medicine is to talk to professionals and to learn about the individual treatments you are considering.

CHAPTER TWO

HERBAL TREATMENTS AND DIETARY SUPPLEMENTS

ELLEN'S STORY

Ellen was overweight and lives with rheumatoid arthritis (painful inflammation of the joints). For three years, she was confined to a wheelchair and continued to gain weight. Because it was so painful for her to move, she was unable to exercise regularly. About the only exercise she got was wheeling herself between her first-floor bedroom and her kitchen. Occasionally, she wheeled herself through the corridors of a shopping mall near her home.

Because of her health, Ellen was unable to work. For several years, she sought help from her family doctor. The doctor prescribed increasing doses of prescription drugs for Ellen's arthritis. Trying to lose weight, Ellen tried a string of crash diets and commercial weight-loss programs. Her doctor tried to persuade her that these diets were potentially harmful. Ellen ignored his advice.

Nothing seemed to work. Ellen's arthritis grew worse, making it too painful for her to get out of bed or to dress herself some days. She suffered from fatigue, fever, and joint swelling, all of which can accompany severe rheumatoid arthritis.

Ellen became depressed over her arthritis and weight gain. Her depression led her to eat more than ever. Her doctor suggested prescription drugs to deal with the depression. But Ellen was reluctant to try them. She said she preferred a natural approach to coping with her mood.

Ellen finally decided to seek the help of a licensed physician trained in alternative-medicine techniques. The physician recommended an herbal treatment to reduce the symptoms of Ellen's arthritis. To deal with Ellen's depression, the specialist suggested small—and temporary—doses of St. John's Wort. The physician persuaded Ellen to follow a healthy, balanced diet. With this diet, Ellen began to eat plenty of fresh fruits and vegetables. She also agreed to begin a program of regular exercise.

After three months, Ellen was feeling much better. Though she still suffered painful bouts of arthritis, she was able to put away her wheelchair and take a part-time office job. She had lost 20 pounds (9 kilograms) and set a goal of losing 30 pounds (14 kg) more over the next year. And best of all, Ellen's depression went away. She began to feel hopeful and optimistic. This, in turn, helped her better cope with her arthritis.

BELINDA'S STORY

Belinda is a software executive. She regularly had trouble falling asleep at night. In the past, she had turned to a prescription sedative or an over-the-counter sleeping pill to be able to go to sleep at night. But the sedatives left her drowsy and listless the next day. She also worried about becoming addicted to the pills.

Belinda decided to try aromatherapy. She proceeded carefully. She started by reading about aromatherapy and talking with her physician. Then she visited a health store that sells herbs and fragrances. There, she bought an essential oil containing sandalwood, which comes from a tree that grows in southeastern Asia and in the Pacific Islands. People who practice aromatherapy believe sandalwood is helpful in creating a sense of calm to help deal with insomnia (trouble sleeping).

Belinda added a few drops of sandalwood oil to her bath water that night. The aroma (scent) relaxed her. Soon after taking the bath, Belinda *was able to fall asleep. In the morning, Belinda didn't know if it was the warm bath, the psychological effect of trying a new approach, or the subtle workings of aromatherapy that had helped her. But she was happy that she had been able to fall asleep without taking a sedative.*

Herbal, or plant, remedies are among the oldest and most frequently used forms of alternative medicine. They are part of a group of alternative treatments that also includes nutritional supplements, fragrances, and specific diets. Often small changes in the intake of nutrients or other substances can bring about major changes in a person's health. Along with regular exercise, this approach can greatly improve well-being.

HERBAL MEDICINE

Coming from aromatic plants, herbs were used in China more than three thousand years ago to treat everything from headaches to difficult pregnancies. According to legend, Chinese emperor Shen Nung wrote the *Pen Tsao Ching* (*The Classic of Herbs*), which listed hundreds of herbal prescriptions. Hundreds of years ago, in medieval Europe, monks planted herb gardens. They studied the medicinal uses of these plants. So did Native American medicine men in the Americas.

Herbs and other vegetation continue to play a role in modern medicine. About one-fourth of all prescription drugs are made from herbs, trees, or other vegetation. Herbal medicines are made from leaves, stems, seeds, and other plant parts. These herbal medicines include teas, syrups, oils, liquid extracts, and dry extracts. Teas are made by soaking dried herbs for a few minutes in hot water or by boiling herbs in water and straining the liquid. For syrups, concentrated extracts are added to sweet-tasting preparations.

These are often used for sore throats and coughs. Oils extracted from plants are often used as rubs for massage, either by themselves or as part of an ointment or cream. Liquid extracts are herbal ingredients dissolved in a liquid (usually water, alcohol, or glycerol). Dry extracts, which are the most concentrated forms of herbal products, are sold as tablets, capsules, or lozenges.

DANGERS OF HERBAL MEDICINE

Herbs contain natural chemicals (active ingredients) that act on specific body systems. Often they work slowly and gently, but not always. If taken in the wrong dose or form, an herbal product can damage body organs and even lead to death. So can herbal products of poor quality.

Herbal remedies should be approached with caution, just as manufactured drugs are. Doctors caution that herbal remedies generally should be avoided by the following people:

- Women who are pregnant or breast-feeding. Any type of medication that can harm the mother will harm the baby as well.
- Any individual undergoing surgery. Herbal remedies can decrease the effectiveness of anesthetics and lead to complications such as high blood pressure.
- People younger than eighteen or older than sixty-five. Individuals in these age ranges process all medications differently.
- Anyone taking other medications. Interactions between herbal and synthetic medications—even over-the-counter painkillers such as aspirin—can cause serious side effects. Be sure to ask a knowledgeable professional, such as your doctor or pharmacist, to avoid unsafe drug-herb interactions.

You should talk to your doctor before taking any herbal remedy. Be aware that some plants have been proven to be dangerous. For example, ephedra was once a popular herbal supplement for losing weight and treating asthma and headaches. But ephedra can lead to heart attacks, seizures, and strokes. For this reason, the sale of ephedra is illegal in the United States. Other potentially dangerous herbs are alpine ragwort, belladonna, bitter orange, kava, licorice, pennyroyal, and wild ginger. Remember to read all labels carefully. Dangerous herbs may be mixed into products that contain a combination of many herbs.

To treat a patient successfully, herbalists must assess thousands of plants for the correct substance, then determine the correct dosage and combination with other herbs. The task is difficult. In recent years, many Western consumers have begun taking herbal supplements to address a wide range of health issues. Scientists caution that the public's zest for herbs could be getting dangerously out of hand. In some cases, the safety and effectiveness of an herbal remedy depend on how the product is processed by the manufacturer and whether the herbs used are of good quality.

GOVERNMENT REGULATIONS

Government regulation of herbal remedies and dietary supplements is loose. This puts both ill and healthy people at risk. Prior to the 1994 Dietary Supplement Health and Education Act (DSHEA), dietary supplements faced the same regulatory requirements as other foods. Under DSHEA, the manufacturer is responsible for determining that its products are safe. The manufacturer must also make sure that its claims about the effectiveness of their products are not false or misleading. This means that dietary supplements do not need approval from FDA before they are marketed.

However, FDA regulations require manufacturers to provide certain information on the labels of dietary supplements. This information includes a descriptive name of the product stating that it is a supplement; the name and place of business of the manufacturer, packer, or distributor; and a complete list of ingredients. Dietary supplements also must have nutrition labeling in the form of a "Supplement Facts" panel. This panel must identify each dietary ingredient in the product. However, unlike makers of prescription drugs, manufacturers of supplements do not have to inform the government about the negative physical effects of their products.

POPULAR HERBAL PRODUCTS

The following are a few of the most popular herbal products in the United States. This list is by no means complete. But it will give you an idea of the uses of some of the products you may see on store shelves.

- **Devil's claw.** This plant of southern Africa, also known as hook plant, gets its name from the small hooks that cover its fruit. The hooks attach to animals as they pass by the plant. In this way, the animals (unknowingly) spread the seeds of the plant. Some believe devil's claw helps people with headaches, back pain, and inflammation in joints to feel better. It has minimal side effects.

- **Echinacea.** This flowering plant is native to the Great Plains region of North America. Echinacea was a favorite of traditional Native American healers. In the twenty-first century, herbal practitioners say that medicinal echinacea stimulates the body's immune system. This, they claim, helps lessen the symptoms of colds and flu. Yet critics fear that echinacea can depress the immune system. They warn that people with human immunodeficiency virus (HIV)—the virus that causes AIDS—should avoid this herb. So should people who have autoimmune diseases, such as lupus or multiple sclerosis.

- **Garlic.** Related to onions, garlic is a common ingredient in many recipes. It also is used to treat a wide range of illnesses and conditions. These include colds and coughs, digestive disorders, and high blood pressure. Garlic can be eaten raw and in other forms, including capsules, tablets, and syrup. Herbal healers says that garlic can lower cholesterol levels and relieve stomach and intestinal problems. However, garlic can produce harmful side effects in some people. It should not be given as medicine to preteen children without first consulting a physician.

- **Ginkgo biloba extract.** The ginkgo tree, native to China, is the only living species of a family of plants that were common about 200 million years ago. The leaves of the ginkgo tree are used to treat circulation problems; brain injury; dizziness; asthma; heart, eye, and ear disorders; and other illnesses. Ginkgo is especially popular in France and Germany. In those countries, people take it in the belief that it improves memory and reduces the likelihood of stroke. However, too much ginkgo could lead to serious physical reactions.

- **Ginseng.** One of the best-known Chinese herbs, ginseng has been used for thousands of years. People often take ginseng for physical and emotional stress, fatigue, fever, and insomnia. Herbal healers claim that ginseng can bolster the immune system and help the liver function better. Ginseng is sold in various forms, including capsules, tablets, and powder. Ginseng can produce serious side effects if taken for too long or in the wrong dosages. People with high blood pressure or heart

Some people take ginseng for ailments, such as fatigue and insomnia. Ginseng has been used for medicinal purposes for thousands of years.

problems should avoid the herb. Some experts warn against taking ginseng for more than a few weeks at a time.

- **Green tea.** Made from the dried leaves of *Camellia sinensis*, people in Asia have drunk green tea for thousands of years. They believe green tea reduces the risk of some cancers and lowers blood cholesterol. While its benefits have not been scientifically proven, green tea is not thought to have serious side effects. Numerous brands can be found on grocery store shelves. However, the best quality green tea is sold in Asian groceries and in specialty tea shops.
- **St. John's Wort.** Used medicinally for more than two thousand years, this herb is promoted in the United States and Europe as a natural cure for mild depression, anxiety, and insomnia.

Life
SECTION D

LIFE.USATODAY.COM

October 8, 2007

From the Pages of USA TODAY

Put the kettle on: It's good for you; Evidence pours in that tea is steeped in health benefits

Tea, something that people around the world enjoy consuming, might actually be good for you.

"The most fascinating thing is, to my knowledge, there is no other natural product known that has such diversified effects," says Hasan Mukhtar, vice chair of dermatology at the University of Wisconsin-Madison.

Health benefits have been attributed to tea, especially green tea, nearly as long as people have been drinking it, Mukhtar and his co-authors write in the July issue of the journal *Life Sciences*. But, they note, scientific investigations of tea and the compounds found in it began less than 30 years ago, and most have been conducted in just the past five years.

Name the ailment, and research suggests tea might protect against it. Most of the studies are either population-based—for example, research shows that prostate cancer is less common in countries where people drink a lot of green tea—or in lab dishes or animals, none of which provide conclusive evidence for humans. But Mukhtar and other tea researchers point

to tea's 5,000-year track record of safety and say at the very least, drinking tea can't hurt, and, most likely, it can help.

Green tea seems to have more health [appeal] than black tea, perhaps because it has been the focus of more research. Although not as well-studied as green tea, black tea probably is at least as beneficial, says Mukhtar, who drinks two cups of black tea and two of green a day.

Tea polyphenols, compounds with antioxidant activity, may protect against heart disease and a variety of cancers, Mukhtar says. His own research has shown that green and black tea, when substituted for drinking water, inhibits the growth of human prostate cancer cells implanted in mice. In addition, Mukhtar has reported that application [on the skin] or [drinking] green tea polyphenols protects against skin cancer in mice.

Human clinical trials by Iman Hakim, a professor at the Arizona Cancer Center at the University of Arizona, suggest that compounds in green tea positively affect genes involved in cancer susceptibility and DNA repair, although not everyone will respond equally well.

Also, Hakim says, an ongoing clinical trial of former and current smokers with chronic obstructive pulmonary disease has found a "significant improvement" in levels of HDL, or good, cholesterol in volunteers given tea as opposed to a placebo drink.

John Foxe says he gives his 3-year-old six or seven cups of milky tea a day. Foxe, professor of neuroscience, biology and psychology at City College of the City University of New York, has conducted clinical trials of theanine, an amino acid in tea that, unlike polyphenols, is small enough to cross the blood/brain barrier. It is present in equal amounts in black, green and oolong teas.

"Probably quite a lot of people have heard tea has cardiovascular effects," says Foxe, whose work was financed by Unilever, maker of Lipton tea. "But that's not why people drink tea. They drink it because it makes them feel good."

Foxe says he has found that as little as 100 milligrams of theanine enabled people to focus better on complicated tasks, but only when consumed with 60 milligrams of caffeine—a combination found in roughly four cups of green tea (which contains half as much caffeine as black).

Just because drinking tea might be good for you doesn't mean adding tea extract to cereal and other foods or to dietary supplements is beneficial. "A lot of that is gimmick," Mukhtar says of products that tout tea extract as an ingredient.

A paper published in April suggests one danger of such products with high

Studies have shown that green tea can have health benefits for those who drink it. But consuming too much green tea extract can have harmful consequences.

doses of green tea extracts. "There are quite a few case reports on liver damage due to taking supplements that contain tea extracts," says biochemist Chung Yang, a Rutgers University [NJ] cancer researcher who co-wrote the paper in the journal *Chemical Research Toxicology*.

Liver function returned to normal when those affected stopped taking the supplements, Yang and his co-authors write. In addition, they say, studies in rodents and dogs suggest that high doses of tea catechins can damage the kidneys and intestine as well as the liver.

Tea drinkers shouldn't worry, though, Yang emphasizes: "It's very clear, there are no published reports concerning toxicity due to tea consumption."

—*Rita Rubin*

(Its name—St. John's Wort—dates back hundreds of years. The plant's flowers bloom in late June, when some Christians celebrate the birth of St. John the Baptist.) It can have negative side effects when combined with prescription drugs such as antidepressants and birth control pills.

DIETARY SUPPLEMENTS

The most important thing to remember about dietary supplements is that they are just that—supplemental. They are not effective unless

Eating for Good Health

The ChooseMyPlate website was created by the United States Department of Agriculture to share the following recommendations for a healthy diet. Check the website (www.ChooseMyPlate.gov) for more information, including how much to eat every day based on your age and gender.

Grains: Of all the grain products (cereal, bread, crackers, rice, or pasta) you eat every day, choose whole grains for at least half of them. Whole grains are things like whole-wheat flour, oatmeal, and brown rice.

Fruits and Vegetables: Choose fruits and vegetables to fill half your plate. Eat a variety of vegetables, including dark green vegetables such as broccoli and spinach; red and orange vegetables such as carrots and sweet potatoes; dried beans and peas (legumes) such as pinto beans and lentils; and starchy vegetables such as corn, lima beans, and green peas. A healthy range of fruits includes berries, apples, bananas, melons, raisins, you eat a healthy diet and get regular exercise. Teenagers have to be especially careful about what they eat. This is because unhealthy habits that start in the teen years can have lifelong consequences. Be sure to avoid fad diets. If you're thinking about becoming vegetarian or vegan, make sure to talk to your family doctor. Your doctor can help you be sure that you're getting all the nutrients you need.

The Food and Nutrition Board was established in 1940. Its Dietary Guidelines for Americans provide guidance for adequate nutrition. Since the 1980s, the guidelines have been published every five years to reflect new scientific findings about healthy eating. Conventional

and citrus fruits such as oranges and grapefruit.

Dairy products: Choose low-fat or fat-free milk, yogurt, and cheese. If you have trouble digesting milk products, choose other calcium sources such as calcium-added orange juice and other beverages to which calcium has been added.

Proteins: Choose low-fat or lean meats, poultry, and fish. Bake, broil, or grill—frying adds fat. Eggs, nuts, and beans are other good sources of protein.

In general, eat only small amounts of butter, margarine, and other shortenings; salty snacks; and sweets. Enjoy your food, but don't overeat. Avoid supersized portions. Check the Nutrition Facts labeling on all processed foods for more information about ingredients. And stay away from saturated fats, trans fats, and sodium, all of which are common ingredients in snacks and other processed foods.

Source: www.ChooseMyPlate.gov

and alternative healers sometimes recommend supplements (such as vitamins) to balance a poor diet; to help people through periods of stress, pregnancy, or other health-related circumstance; to help ward off illness; or to help with the effects of aging.

Essential nutrients for a healthy diet include proteins, which are made up of organic compounds called amino acids; vitamins and minerals such as calcium and iron; and fats and carbohydrates. These nutrients occur naturally in foods. Supplements can increase the amount of these compounds in the body.

Nutritional and dietary supplements are available over the counter at pharmacies or grocery stores, through the mail and the Internet, and even by prescription. Under U.S. law, a dietary supplement is a product that fits the following criteria:

- It is intended to supplement, not replace, a healthy diet.
- It contains one or more dietary ingredients (including vitamins, minerals, herbs or plant products, amino acids, and certain other substances) in some form.
- It is intended to be taken by mouth, in forms such as tablets, capsules, powder, softgel, gelcap, or liquid.
- It is labeled as a dietary supplement.

It is important to take a commonsense approach to nutritional and dietary supplements. Remember that the claim that a product is "natural" does not make it safe. Alcohol, nicotine, and the narcotic in cocaine, for example, are natural substances. But they can do great damage to a person's health.

You should also be aware that some nutritional and dietary supplements can cause great harm. For example, large doses of vitamins A and D can damage the liver. Taking too much vitamin B_6 can lead to nerve damage. In addition, taking too much of a supplementary nutrient can interact with other nutrients in the body. This cancels out the healthy effects of a nutrient. For example, too much calcium can lead to iron deficiency. Too much zinc can interfere with the absorption of copper in the body.

Don't buy into trendy weight-loss diets, megavitamin therapies, or unproven claims by herbal remedy promoters or makers of other controversial nutritional supplements. Check first with an expert so you don't invite more problems than solutions. The bottom line: eat right, consider taking a high-quality multiple vitamin each day, and follow the advice of a qualified physician or dietary specialist. This is the wisest approach to maintaining good health.

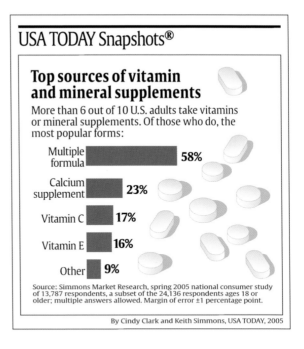

USA TODAY Snapshots®

Top sources of vitamin and mineral supplements

More than 6 out of 10 U.S. adults take vitamins or mineral supplements. Of those who do, the most popular forms:

- Multiple formula — **58%**
- Calcium supplement — **23%**
- Vitamin C — **17%**
- Vitamin E — **16%**
- Other — **9%**

Source: Simmons Market Research, spring 2005 national consumer study of 13,787 respondents, a subset of the 24,136 respondents ages 18 or older; multiple answers allowed. Margin of error ±1 percentage point.

By Cindy Clark and Keith Simmons, USA TODAY, 2005

AROMATHERAPY

Aromatherapy is the use of fragrant oils extracted from herbs, flowers, and fruits to create a sense of well-being. The oils can be placed in a reed diffuser—rattan reeds placed with aromatherapy oils into a glass jar or vase. The reeds naturally suck up the oil, which then evaporates into the air that you breathe. The oils can also be massaged into the skin or added to bath water. Aromatic candles are another common form of aromatherapy.

August 5, 2010

From the Pages of USA TODAY

High risk of supplements gets exposed—yet again

Our view: Yes, some work. Others are useless or worse. Safety? Not easily found.

"We Americans do love our dietary supplements," says the watchdog publication *Consumer Reports* in its latest issue. And indeed we do: The craving for pills, potions and powders as a quick fix for [many] concerns about health and well-being has created a $27 billion industry. That's roughly as much as the nation spends each year on shoes.

And, as *Consumer Reports* points out, while many users believe that sale of unsafe or ineffective supplements must be illegal, it is not. The public has little protection from useless, fraudulent [false], dangerous or even deadly products, thanks to special protection Congress gave the industry in 1994.

Want to ease your aches and pains? Lose weight? Improve your prowess on the athletic field or in the bedroom? The supplements industry has something for you, even if it has never been subjected to any credible scientific testing, even if tests that have been conducted show it to be useless, even if it has ingredients that might come from tainted sources or uninspected factories in China, even if it's touted as "natural" but in fact includes undisclosed chemical ingredients, including some that have been banned by law because they are dangerous and others that could mix badly with other medications you're taking.

Fragrant plants have had a place in healing practices for thousands of years. Evidence of the use of aromatherapy exists from ancient civilizations in China, India, Egypt, and Rome. The history of modern aromatherapy began in the 1930s, when French chemist René-

The *Consumer Reports* analysis spotlights a list of 12 widely used supplement ingredients linked to serious health risks, including cardiovascular, liver and kidney problems.

Little of this is new. Congress's Government Accountability Office and studies ordered by congressional committees and various private organizations have shown repeatedly that [taking] supplements can be a game of chance. Though in some cases, a supplement could help, in others its only visible impact will be on your wallet, and in a few instances it might have [dangerous] consequences.

On top of the [many] supplement-use horror stories recorded over the years, many of which we've cited in previous editorials on this subject, *Consumer Reports* offers more:

- A Tennessee man who took a health supplement developed diarrhea, joint pain, hair loss and lung problems, and lost his fingernails and toenails. The distributor eventually recalled the product but is fighting its former customer in court.
- A student-athlete who bought a performance supplement online that claimed to be "legal" wound up in the hospital with liver failure due to the [illegal] steroid it included; the illness caused him to lose an athletic scholarship.
- An Oklahoma woman bought a treatment for Lyme disease that turned her skin blue.

Spokesmen for the self-described "responsible" part of the industry claim that the limited powers given the Food and Drug Administration [FDA] are adequate to protect the public. But the record says otherwise. It's so hard for FDA to ban a product that only one such case has ever succeeded. That effort, involving ephedrine alkaloids, dragged on for years while weight-loss products that included ephedra were implicated in thousands of illnesses and some deaths.

Consumer Reports advises the public to be skeptical of claims made for supplements in ads, on TV and by pill-store sales staff. But people will always yearn for a magic [cure], which is why supplements, like drugs, shouldn't be allowed on store shelves till they've been proven safe and effective.

—USA TODAY editors

Maurice Gattefossé coined the term *aromathérapie*. He studied the effects of essential oils on physical and mental healing.

According to aromatherapy theory, when the scent of an essential oil is inhaled, molecules in the oil stimulate the olfactory system in the nasal passages. The olfactory glands interact with the brain's limbic system. The seat of emotional experience in the brain, the limbic system also controls such functions as heart rate, breathing, hormone production, memory, and breathing. The essential oils are believed to have a direct psychological and physical effect. When massaged directly on the skin, molecules of the essential oils are said to interact with the nervous system. In some cases, they are said to interact directly with tissues that need healing.

Critics of aromatherapy say that scientific research does not support its powers of healing. Aromatherapy, they claim, may be little more than the power of suggestion at work. Many people associate specific smells with events or moods, the critics argue. For this reason, it is little wonder that a fragrance can affect a person's mood or physical well-being. But the idea that one specific aroma will produce exactly the same effect in all people is doubtful, the

Rosemary is a popular aromatherapy oil. It is said to be good for muscular pain.

critics say. After all, one person may have a pleasing memory of a fragrance such as lavender. Another person may associate it with an unpleasant experience.

The following is a list of a few of the most popular aromatherapy oils and conditions for which they are used:

- **Lavender:** headaches, insomnia
- **Peppermint:** digestive disorders
- **Rosemary:** muscular pain
- **Sandalwood:** depression, anxiety, insomnia
- **Tea tree:** respiratory problems, acne, dandruff

Some people, such as those with allergies, may experience reactions to certain oils, such as skin irritation and respiratory discomfort. Some products that can cause these side effects are eucalyptus, ginger, cinnamon, and some citrus oils. And remember, essential oils should never be swallowed or applied undiluted to the skin.

CHAPTER THREE

THE MIND-BODY CONNECTION

LATISHA'S STORY

L atisha is intelligent. But she always had trouble concentrating in school. By the time she was in junior high, her grades in math, English, and science were suffering. Many days, her teachers would catch her staring out the classroom window or doodling in her notebook.

Latisha knew she had a problem. When she was eight years old, her mother had taken her to a psychologist. She diagnosed Latisha's difficulty as attention deficit hyperactivity disorder, or ADHD.

ADHD is common among children. Many adults struggle with it too. Typically, people living with ADHD find it difficult to stay focused at school or at work. They often have trouble managing and remembering important assignments and responsibilities.

For several years after her diagnosis, Latisha took a drug called Ritalin. But her problems in school didn't go away. Eventually, her mother became worried that taking the drug over a long period of time might have side effects for Latisha that would be worse than ADHD itself. So Latisha's mother did some research into alternative therapies. She read an article about hypnotherapy. Latisha's mother was interested in this approach. She asked a school guidance counselor about it. The counselor referred Latisha's mother to Jack, a hypnotist who practiced nearby.

Jack wondered whether Latisha actually had ADHD. He explained to Latisha and her mom that many young people are incorrectly diagnosed with ADHD. What looks like ADHD can sometimes be a behavioral problem caused by an allergy. It can also be a dietary deficiency or a mineral imbalance in the young person's system. Jack also said that people who do have ADHD often can learn to manage the disorder without drugs. They can do this by tapping into their own internal powers. He suggested hypnosis as a safe way to unlock those powers.

Latisha and her mother decided to give hypnosis a try. Jack spent part of the first session making sure that Latisha was ready for and open to treatment. He explained the process to Latisha and her mother. He talked with Latisha about her physical and mental health. He explained that Latisha would be fully aware of her surroundings during hypnosis. He also made sure Latisha knew that hypnosis would not make her do anything against her will or anything that would embarrass her. Jack made sure that Latisha felt safe and comfortable with him. Latisha then began her first session of hypnosis therapy.

Jack asked Latisha to relax in a reclining chair as he spoke to her in a slow, soothing voice. He asked Latisha to imagine herself walking down a long country lane on a bright fall day, guiding her to a state of deep concentration and relaxation. Then Jack started talking to Latisha about school. He made suggestions about how to focus on her schoolwork and recommended some specific techniques for her to think about.

In the next session, Jack started to talk about the underlying causes of Latisha's attention problems. He asked her to describe her fears and concerns about competing academically with her friends and siblings. He explained that those fears might negatively affect her progress in school.

Latisha spoke of an older brother who had done well in high school and college. This brother had gone on to medical school. She also spoke of her younger sister. At the age of seven, this sister already was a budding actress in a local theater group.

Latisha said she was worried about not measuring up to the successes of her sister and brother. In making that discovery, Jack started focusing on Latisha's concerns. He helped her analyze her strengths and her weaknesses. After the session, he spoke with Latisha's mother about *providing support to help Latisha build up her self-esteem.*

Latisha had five more sessions of hypnotherapy. Her grades at school improved a lot. After consulting with her psychologist, Latisha was able to stop taking Ritalin. At times, Latisha still has trouble focusing and concentrating. But in the evenings, after a day when she catches herself lacking concentration, she uses a self-hypnosis technique that Jack taught her. This technique helps her refocus on her schoolwork. After a while, Latisha is able to get herself back on track and complete her assignments.

Just as importantly, Latisha has been able to recognize that she is unfairly comparing herself to her siblings. In time, she has come to see herself as a unique person with amazing talents and interests all her own.

NATHAN'S STORY

Nathan was a truck driver who had never had any major health issues. But one morning, just after the sun rose, he collapsed in the parking lot of a truck stop. His right arm was paralyzed, his vision was blurred, and his speech was slurred. Luckily for Nathan, another trucker saw him collapse and called 9-1-1. After some tests, the doctors confirmed what Nathan already suspected. Nathan had had a mild stroke.

In a few days, Nathan was able to speak clearly again. But he still could not use his right arm. His doctor told him that hypertension—high blood pressure—put him at great risk of another stroke. To help address both problems—Nathan's paralyzed arm and high blood pressure— Nathan's doctor prescribed drugs. He also recommended that Nathan go on a low-salt diet and do physical therapy. Lastly, Nathan's doctor also suggested that he try biofeedback. Nathan would work with a trained biofeedback professional to control his body with the powers of his own mind.

Nathan followed his doctor's advice for his arm and blood pressure problems. In dealing with his health, Nathan relied on the same energy and long-term concentration he needed as a long-distance truck driver. He knew that the success of his biofeedback program would also depend on this same willpower and on a positive attitude.

The work, both conventional and alternative, was not easy. Nathan came close to giving up. But the health-care workers at the biofeedback clinic, along with his wife, medical doctor, and physical therapists, supported Nathan. They helped him see that his physical body—once thought to be beyond the influence of the mind—is something he can consciously control.

Patients undergoing biofeedback can tell from the sensors what is happening inside their bodies.

Over several months, Nathan learned to control his blood pressure. He also began to feel sensation in his arm again. And after learning how to work with the damaged arm muscles, he began to regain some use of his arm.

RYAN'S STORY

When Ryan was eleven years old, he was brutally beaten and sexually assaulted by a man in his neighborhood. This traumatic event caused Ryan to stop communicating with people around him. Ryan soon began showing other signs of mental illness—depression, compulsive behavior, and aggression toward anyone who tried to get close to or talk to him.

Ryan's mental health got worse and worse. After a few months, he ended up in a hospital unit for the mentally ill. The doctors and counselors there had no luck in their efforts to break through Ryan's wall of silence and anger. For many months, Ryan's situation seemed hopeless.

One day a caseworker on Ryan's unit noticed something important. Ryan was in his room, curled up on his bed in a fetal position, his face turned toward the wall. The sounds of classical piano music could be heard from a room down the hall. Ryan turned and lay on his back, opened his eyes, and began moving gently to the music. When the music stopped abruptly—a nurse had closed the door of the room from which the sound came—Ryan again turned toward the wall. His body became tight and motionless. This gave the caseworker a clue about how to get through to Ryan.

She consulted with Ryan's treatment team. The team included a specialist trained in the field of music therapy. This discipline uses music to achieve nonmusical goals. These goals may be to ease pain, soothe anxiety, treat people with physical or mental disabilities, or comfort those who are terminally ill.

In Ryan's case, the goal was to use music to try to draw him out of his emotional shell. Music therapy would also give him a means of self-expression and a safe way for him to release his pent-up anger and fear. Over time, Ryan became less withdrawn and more expressive. The music did not cure his emotional trauma or remove the pain he felt. But it provided a way for him to begin to recover from his terrible experience. It also offered a way for him to relate to people around him.

Mind-body therapies include guided imagery, hypnosis, biofeedback, meditation, music and art therapy, yoga, tai chi, and qigong (see chapter 6 for more on qigong). When people get sick, the first impulse is often to look for a physical cause. But sometimes, illness and healing are mysterious. Conventional science and direct observation can't always discover obvious causes and cures.

Researchers still aren't sure how much the mind can affect the body or how people can use the mind-body connection to prevent or overcome illness. Some believe that emotions such as fear, hopelessness, optimism, and courage have a lot to do with whether a person can recover quickly from illness. Conventional medicine tends to focus on the visible and measurable aspects of health. Mind-body medicine makes a connection between physical healing and a person's thoughts, feelings, and beliefs.

For example, many scientists believe that emotions can bring on chemical changes in the body. For this reason, experts are looking for new ways to treat illnesses, such as cancer and heart disease. They hope these new methods can use the power of the mind and of emotions to help people who are sick.

Like all integrative medicine, mind-body therapies put the patient—not the physician—at the center of the healing process. This does not mean that a patient can control every illness. However, a growing number of medical researchers believe that a patient's emotions and outlook can have an important effect on the life of an illness. They believe that the tools of conventional Western medicine, such as surgery and prescription drugs, may be just one part of the healing process.

A major research breakthrough in mind-body medicine came in the 1970s. Robert Ader, director of the Division of Behavioral and Psychosocial Medicine at the University of Rochester (New York) School of Medicine, was working with immunologist Nicholas Cohen. They discovered that the immune system can learn to respond to conditioning. Ader found that rats, whose illness-fighting powers are similar to those of humans, could be conditioned to suppress their

February 4, 2008

From the Pages of USA TODAY

Healing vs. hooey
Alternative therapies are put under the microscope

Biostatistician R. Barker Bausell tried acupuncture once, for a chronic backache. The needle pricks and the warmth from the heat lamp aimed at his sore back felt good at the time, he recalls. They didn't do a thing for his underlying pain.

But when the acupuncturist asked if the treatment had helped, Bausell said yes. "What could I say? I worked with the guy all the time," says the scientist, who was then director of research at a center for complementary medicine at the University of Maryland.

Today, Bausell is saying plenty about his five years in the world of complementary and alternative medicine (also known as CAM). He has written a book called *Snake Oil Science: The Truth About Complementary and Alternative Medicine*.

In it, he uses a broad brush to paint doubt over therapies that include acupuncture, herbal medicine, homeopathy, chiropractic treatment, hypnosis and energy healing, among others. An obvious criticism is that he lumps together very different approaches.

But he argues that the differences aren't as important as what they share: an ability to make people feel better—if patients believe they will. In short, Bausell writes: "CAM recipients feel better because of the placebo effect."

Can that be universally true? If it is, then the National Institutes of Health is spending $121 million a year to study the placebo effect at its National Center for Complementary and Alternative Medicine. And many leading medical centers are offering placebos, too, thanks in part to that federal research money—and huge patient demand.

immune systems in response to the sweet taste of saccharin.

Ader played a key role in establishing the field of psychoneuroimmunology (PNI). This field examines the link between the immune system and the behavioral, nervous system,

Bausell offers a different perspective, one not shared by all scientists. But whether his broad condemnation is fair, his description of factors that might underlie and [increase] the placebo effect (the ability of sham treatments to relieve symptoms) is thought-provoking. Among them:

- The patient/provider bond. It's no mistake, Bausell says, that alternative providers often seem especially caring. That connection helps convince patients that treatments will work—and may even lead polite patients to exaggerate or lie about improvement (as Bausell once did).
- The "Hawthorne effect." This effect is at play when patients improve health habits in response to close medical attention. (It's named for a power plant whose workers became more productive when observed for a study.) So the arthritis patient getting acupuncture also takes her prescription drugs more regularly, but credits the needles when her pain [goes away].
- The natural history of illness. Many conditions [come and go] or tend to improve over time. But treatment, not time, may get the credit.
- Mistaken memories. People who believe a therapy helps may remember their initial symptoms as more intense than they actually were—a mental trick that makes current symptoms seem milder.
- Pride. Patients and practitioners alike have a strong need to believe they've made smart choices.

Of course, all of these factors can be at work in conventional medicine, too. Luckily, Bausell says, the true effectiveness of any treatment can be sorted out by well-designed, rigorously reviewed and repeated studies that compare that treatment to placebos. When CAM treatments undergo that kind of study, he claims, they usually work—but only as well as the placebos. Typically, he says, that means any improvement is temporary and mild. Occasionally, a good study shows a CAM therapy working better than placebos, he says, but he chalks that up to statistical chance.

Bausell doesn't expect to dissuade true believers, though: "People like stories better than statistics. If a friend says they've tried something and it works, it has a much stronger effect than any study."

For more on the research: nccam.nih.gov.

—Kim Painter

and hormone functions of the body. PNI researchers have found that the immune system, once thought to work on its own, is affected by the brain. Scientists have come to believe that the mind is closely linked to many bodily functions. They do not totally understand how.

MIND-BODY SCAMS

Of course, mind-body medicine has limits and risks, just as other medical approaches do. Relying only on the mind to heal the body can give patients false hope. It can persuade them to say no to conventional therapies that could prolong their lives or cure a disease.

The mental strain of illness sometimes causes people to turn to false healers. These people prey on the sick, claiming they have the power to heal, even though they do not have medical training. Dr. David Felten of the Beaumont Research Institute in Royal Oak, Michigan, notes that "a lot of us in [medicine] tend to be [very] conservative because of the [false healers] who figure, what have they got to lose? They prey on the desperate, and the elderly, and the dying, promising them all kinds of cures if only they follow their remedy, for the low, low price of whatever it turns out to be—all without any substantiation [proof] whatsoever."

People with cancer are prime targets for scams that try to get patients to reject traditional Western medicine in favor of unproven alternative therapies. Alternative therapies can help people cope with pain. They can also help control the side effects, such as nausea and weakness, that come with conventional cancer treatments. Mind-body therapy cannot cure cancer, however. For this reason, cancer patients should avoid mind-body therapists who pressure them to stop treatments prescribed by their medical team. This is especially true in the twenty-first century, when many medical doctors include alternative methods such as meditation and massage in treatment plans for their cancer patients.

Another risk of mind-body medicine is that patients may believe that their body is completely under their mental control. They believe that their illness is just a sign of some sort of mental weakness. It is important to remember that scientists have much to learn about the connection between the brain (mind) and illness (body). All the same, no responsible practitioner would jump to the conclusion that a physical illness has only a mental cause.

SPIRITUALITY AND HEALING

Caregivers within conventional medicine are beginning to rely more on the mind-body connection for healing. For example, at the Emmanuel Unit of St. Francis Hospital in Greenville, South Carolina, caregivers have used music therapy and prayer along with conventional treatments to help patients. And the Lutheran Theological Southern Seminary in South Carolina joined with the University of South Carolina School of Public Health in a national project. Paid for by the Carter Center in Atlanta, Georgia, the project's goal was to find programs that bring together religious and medical professionals to improve training.

A growing number of studies suggest that prayer can positively impact health and healing. No one yet knows exactly how, and not all scientific studies come to the same conclusions. But this type of research is part of a growing body of science that is examining how the mind—through conscious thought and unconscious brain activity—can impact physical health.

GUIDED IMAGERY

Ancient Egyptians and ancient Greeks used visualization as a method of healing. And modern medical research has shown that mental images affect physical health. Visualizing, or imagining, a beautiful, calm landscape or remembering a happy moment can actually help reduce physical and emotional pain. These pleasant images cause the brain to send messages to the body that can help lessen symptoms.

USA TODAY
Life
SECTION D
LIFE.USATODAY.COM

August 5, 2009

From the Pages of USA TODAY

Fighting postwar stress

Groups, congregations pave a path of spirituality to help veterans

Hopelessness haunted Tim Pollock for years after an Iraqi [rebel soldier] blew off half his skull during a [military] operation in 2004. Back home in Columbiana, Ohio, the retired Army infantryman drank hard, bought a gun and considered suicide.

But today Pollock, 30, has a renewed sense of purpose despite his seizures and other war-related disabilities. He visits soldiers in hospitals. He coaches veterans who struggle as he does with agitation, anxiety and other symptoms of post-traumatic stress disorder (PTSD). And he's studying for the ministry.

"I'll always have post-traumatic stress, but I'm learning through God how to control that," says Pollock, who leads a veteran support group through Point Man International Ministries, an independent non-profit [organization]. "I'm learning how to change my feelings of anger into feelings of love and help people with their problems."

As soldiers return home from Iraq and Afghanistan, congregations are discovering how spirituality can help veterans with postwar stress. But many pastors remain unsure how to help when veterans deal with chronic nightmares, outbursts and panic attacks.

An army of helpers

Several ministries are trying.

- Since 2007, Campus Crusade for Christ's Military Ministry has helped about 100 local churches launch or expand programs addressing spiritual needs that accompany PTSD.
- Point Man support groups, led by veterans and supported by local congregations, have grown from 219 in

The practice of guided imagery uses memories, dreams, and fantasies to control chronic pain. It can also control blood pressure and reduce stress. Research shows that practicing guided imagery

2007 to 250 today. Iraq and Afghanistan war veterans now make up 20% of attendees, up from just 1% in 2007, says Point Man president Dana Morgan.

- Other groups have launched grassroots efforts, such as the Coming Home Collaborative, a 3-year-old network of Minneapolis [MN]-area Lutheran congregations.

Nearly 20% of service members who have returned from Iraq and Afghanistan report symptoms of PTSD or major depression, yet fewer than half seek treatment, a Rand Corp. study found last year. Women with the disorder often go undiagnosed, in part because they're wrongly presumed to be less susceptible in non-combat roles, said a report in July from the Defense Centers of Excellence for Psychological Health and Traumatic Brain Injury.

PTSD poses challenges because it is often hidden. A veteran with the disorder may appear fine in worship, but at home he may obsess about security, struggle to sleep, panic at loud noises or become easily enraged. Such symptoms [show up] in certain trauma survivors, including some who have experienced the horrors of war up close, says Matthew Friedman of the National Center for Post-Traumatic Stress Disorder in the Department of Veteran Affairs.

For some congregations, PTSD ministries are largely about raising awareness.

At Calvary United Methodist Church in Colorado Springs [CO], where most members have a military connection, leaders have been trained to spot symptoms and refer those affected, especially family members, to counselors.

Other congregations are tackling what they see as the disorder's spiritual dimension. Skyway Church in Goodyear, Ariz., launched a support group last year for veterans and one for family members. John Blehm, a Vietnam War veteran and PTSD patient who leads the support group, says military clinicians "do not address the spiritual wounds of our troops."

"Many will feel guilty for the inhumane things they have done in order to survive in war," Blehm says. "Once they understand they are not alone and can be forgiven, then healing begins."

Cautious steps forward

Friedman says clergy can help facilitate connections among veterans or address spiritual dimensions, such as guilt or reconciliation. "People really don't like to go to a psychiatric clinic unless they have to," Friedman says.

"We emphasize that everybody else can forgive you, and now it's your turn to forgive yourself because God already has," Morgan says. "And then we go from there."

—G. Jeffrey MacDonald

before surgery can help reduce fear and anxiety. Some people use guided imagery to improve their performance in a sporting event or when playing a musical instrument.

A person practicing guided imagery uses his or her imagination to "see" a beautiful place or recall soothing memories. To be successful with this method, it is best to start by using an instructional CD. Or you can find a professional with experience in imagery techniques. After a few sessions, many people are able to practice imagery on their own, without guidance.

A session of guided imagery usually lasts from about fifteen to thirty minutes. The four basic steps are these:

1. **Relax**. Wear loose-fitting clothing and sit or lie down in a comfortable, quiet place. Begin taking slow, deep breaths.
2. **Concentrate**. Focus attention on your breathing, not your thoughts, to clear your mind.
3. **Visualize**. In a guided session, the leader will describe a scene, such as a remote mountainside or a quiet stream. If you are practicing on your own, picture a special, safe place that you love. Think about this place and the positive feelings it brings you for as long as you like.
4. **End the session**. When you are ready, slowly open your eyes. Take a deep breath to come back to the present. You will feel relaxed and refreshed.

HYPNOSIS

Like guided imagery, hypnosis is a form of highly focused concentration. It is commonly used to help people control addictions and to cope with behavioral problems such as attention deficit disorder. It can also help people increase their ability to concentrate on schoolwork or other tasks. Hypnosis can help people sleep better, deal with chronic pain, and lose some of their fear of dental procedures.

Sometimes hypnosis is used along with conventional medical treatment. Instead of relying on a chemical anesthetic for a tooth extraction, for example, a patient may be able to block out the pain of the procedure under the guidance of a hypnotist.

Hypnotism works by making a person highly open to suggestion. However, no one can be hypnotized against his or her wishes. The aim of hypnosis is to put the conscious mind at rest and to activate the unconscious mind. A typical treatment session begins with the hypnotist asking the person to relax. Then, at the suggestion of the hypnotist (or yourself, if you are doing self-hypnosis), attention is shifted away from the immediate surroundings. You will then focus on a specific object, place, or idea.

During hypnosis, you are not asleep. In fact, the hypnotized person is very aware of his or her surroundings. The hypnotist cannot make you do anything that goes against your beliefs or that would embarrass you. You may also choose not to respond to a suggestion from the hypnotist if you don't want to.

Hypnosis can be used as treatment to help people with everything from addictions to behavioral problems.

Anyone has the potential to be hypnotized. However, the degree to which a person can be hypnotized varies with each person. If you go to a hypnotist, be sure that person has had thorough training and has the approval of an organization such as the National Guild of Hypnotists or the American Society of Clinical Hypnosis.

BIOFEEDBACK

Biofeedback trains people to use willpower, deep relaxation, and other techniques to control the body voluntarily. Through biofeedback, a person can control bodily functions such as temperature, heart rate, blood pressure, and muscle contraction. The technique also can help control asthma symptoms, urinary incontinence, migraine headaches, and chronic pain. Often, biofeedback is used to bring on deep relaxation. This helps improve the effectiveness of other therapies and may help ward off illness or stress. Sessions first take place in a therapist's office. The goal is to teach patients eventually to control these functions on their own.

The principles of biofeedback are hundreds, if not thousands, of years old. In ancient China, healers could regulate heart rate, blood pressure, skin temperature, and other bodily functions not normally thought to be under conscious control. Experimentation on modern biofeedback began in the mid-1900s. In the early 1940s, researchers in the United States and Britain developed equipment to detect tiny physical responses in the body. By the late 1960s, researchers in the United States had demonstrated that the method had therapeutic uses. Soon biofeedback clinics were springing up from coast to coast.

Among the pioneers of biofeedback research were Elmer and Alyce Green, of the Menninger Foundation in Topeka, Kansas. In the early 1960s, the Greens took a woman's skin temperature to chart her physiological changes during relaxation exercises. The Greens noticed that the woman's hand temperature suddenly rose 10 degrees. The woman told them that a migraine headache she'd been feeling went away at that same moment. From that experience, the Greens went on to develop a biofeedback temperature device. They taught people how to ease migraine headaches by using relaxation exercises to raise their hand temperatures. The link between hand temperature and headache pain pointed to an important idea. If a person could learn to control a biological function such as body temperature, pain and other disorders might be controlled.

HOW DOES BIOFEEDBACK WORK?

A biofeedback practitioner attaches electrodes (sensors) to the skin. These sensors send information to a computer that monitors body functions. The information received (feedback) registers on the computer screen. The computer gives off a tone or displays a visual cue (change in brightness or a line moving across a grid). When Nathan visited a therapist for his hypertension, electrodes attached to his skin measured his blood pressure, heart rate, and other metabolic functions. These readings allowed Nathan to keep track of his blood pressure. Through subtle physical, emotional, and mental adjustments, he learned to regulate it.

Usually, people cannot tell when their blood pressure has changed. But the sensors gave Nathan clues about what was happening in his heart, arteries, and veins. The device measured the temperature of his skin. It detected fluctuations in blood flow from the changes it measured in the expansion and contraction of Nathan's blood vessels. A finger pulse measured his pulse rate and blood flow (his heart activity), giving clues as to whether he was anxious or nervous.

When Nathan's blood pressure dropped below a certain target level, the biofeedback device gave off a tone. This sound told him that he had achieved his blood pressure goal. With practice he could learn to help control stress—often a factor in high blood pressure—by altering his brain waves.

Nathan's therapist used the same approach to try to regain use of Nathan's disabled arm. In a process known as electromyographic biofeedback, the therapist attached electrodes to Nathan's arm. The electrodes monitor electrical impulses in the muscles. As Nathan tried to use the arm, the therapist told him he would be able to tell how successful he was by watching the monitor. Over time, Nathan learned to engage the muscles. He learned to influence their contractions and expansions, using the biofeedback monitor as a guide.

MEDITATION

Biofeedback requires technology. Meditation, on the other hand, is a solitary, contemplative discipline. It can be practiced in any setting. Over the centuries, people of many religions—including Buddhism, Hinduism, Christianity, and Islam—have practiced meditation as part of their spiritual beliefs. But you can meditate even if you do not follow a particular faith or spiritual philosophy. In the United States, meditation in

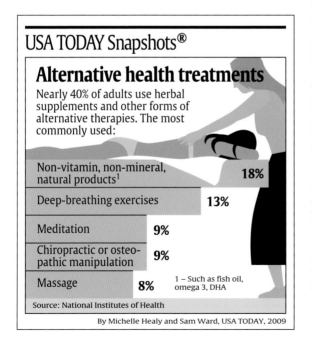

USA TODAY Snapshots®

Alternative health treatments

Nearly 40% of adults use herbal supplements and other forms of alternative therapies. The most commonly used:

Non-vitamin, non-mineral, natural products[1]	18%
Deep-breathing exercises	13%
Meditation	9%
Chiropractic or osteopathic manipulation	9%
Massage	8%

1 – Such as fish oil, omega 3, DHA

Source: National Institutes of Health

By Michelle Healy and Sam Ward, USA TODAY, 2009

nonreligious settings is an increasingly popular method to control stress.

You can think of meditation as a mental state of peace and heightened awareness. You create this state of being by contemplating an object, idea, image, mantra (a repeated phrase), or the rhythm of your breath. You can also create this state by clearing your mind of thought. Meditation can have many physical and emotional benefits. These include less muscle tension, a lower heart rate, and a change in brain-wave patterns—all of which signal a state of deep relaxation.

Meditation is used by many people in the United States to try to control stress.

A pioneer in mind-body medicine is Dr. Herbert Benson. In the late 1960s, Dr. Benson (then at Harvard University and later the director of the Benson-Henry Institute for Mind Body Medicine in Massachusetts) was studying stress in humans. He discovered that activating certain areas of the brain results in reducing stress. Dr. Benson referred to this reaction as the relaxation response. This response is a physical state of deep rest that changes how the body reacts to stress. Benson supports meditation as a way to create the relaxation response. During the relaxation response, these changes take place in the body:

- The metabolism decreases.
- The heart rate slows and muscles relax.
- Breathing becomes slower.
- Blood pressure decreases.

The preferred method of meditation, which is practiced at the Benson-Henry Institute, follows these steps:

1. Pick a focus word, short phrase, or prayer that is firmly rooted in your belief system. The word or phrase might be something like *one, peace, Hail Mary full of grace, shalom*, or *om*.
2. Sit quietly in a comfortable position.
3. Close your eyes.
4. Relax your muscles, progressing from your feet to your calves, thighs, abdomen, shoulders, head, and neck.
5. Breathe slowly and naturally. As you breathe, say your focus word, sound, phrase, or prayer silently to yourself as you exhale.
6. Have a passive attitude. Don't worry about how well you're doing. When other thoughts come to mind, simply say to yourself, "Oh well," and gently return to the silent repetition of your word, phrase, or sound.
7. Continue for ten to twenty minutes.
8. As you are ready to end your meditation, do not stand up immediately. Continue sitting quietly for a minute or so. Allow other thoughts to return to your mind. Then open your eyes. Sit quietly for another minute before rising.
9. Practice the technique once or twice daily. Good times to do so are before breakfast and before dinner.

MUSIC THERAPY

The field of music therapy is not new. The Chinese have used it for thousands of years. Ancient Greek thinkers such as Aristotle, Plato, and Pythagoras recognized music's healing power.

In the United States, music therapy is a health profession. Certified practitioners of music therapy must meet national standards. The field gained popularity in the 1940s. During World War II (1939–1945), some soldiers received music therapy to manage their combat-related stress. After the war, in 1950, the National Association for Music Therapy was established. Many universities offer formal programs of study in the discipline.

Some researchers say that music therapy can have a direct effect on a person's physiological processes, such as heart rate and the release of pain-killing chemicals in the brain. Yet it remains unclear how music brings about those changes. What is clear, however, is that music can have great therapeutic value. The potential benefits

Music therapy is used along with conventional medicine in some hospitals to help patients cope with pain and emotional distress.

include improving a patient's mood and drawing that person into contact with other people. The benefits can also include creating an outlet for emotional expression and providing a means of improving memory and physical flexibility.

MUSIC THERAPY HOW-TO

In a music therapy session, the therapist will first determine what kinds of music the patient responds to. In Ryan's case, the therapist confirmed what the counselor had noticed. Ryan seemed to prefer classical music, and Mozart seemed to be his favorite composer.

The therapist saw subtle changes in Ryan when he heard the music. She could soon anticipate what tones and rhythms would appeal to him the most. One day she experienced a huge breakthrough in Ryan's therapy. He quietly asked her to replay a part of the music he had heard earlier in the session.

Eventually, Ryan chose the selections he wanted the therapist to play. The rapport between them grew to a point that Ryan could begin speaking about the emotions locked up inside him.

As she drew him out, the therapist gave Ryan some musical instruments to play. He started with a drum at first and later played a small electronic keyboard. Ryan had never had musical training. But he beat the drum in regular and powerful beats, sometimes showing signs of anger as he swung the drumstick harder and harder. Often, Ryan would simply slide the stick over the skin of the drum in gentle movements. He would close his eyes for long periods of time, his face set in a grimace.

One day, Ryan asked to bring the keyboard to a group meeting of emotionally disturbed young people. With much fanfare, he played a tune for the gathering. This was a sign of emotional healing—the first sign that Ryan was able to reach out to others on his own.

YOGA

The word *yoga* comes from a Sanskrit term (*yunatki*) meaning "to join." It is a Hindu spiritual practice that started thousands of years ago in India. The goal of yoga is to reach complete peacefulness of mind and body through a series of physical poses (asanas) and concentration on breathing (*pranayama*). Yoga has become very popular in the United States. Most people who practice yoga in the United States and other Western cultures do not focus on spiritual goals. They use the poses and breathing routines to release stress, increase flexibility, and calm the mind.

Yoga can help reduce symptoms of a number of health problems, including anxiety, asthma, back pain, depression, and high blood pressure. Yoga can be practiced alone or in a group setting. Risks

Yoga is an ancient spiritual practice that started in India. In the twenty-first century, most people who practice yoga in the United States do it for stress relief and to increase flexibility.

Life
SECTION D
LIFE.USATODAY.COM

August 19, 2010

From the Pages of USA TODAY

Study: Tai chi could ease fibromyalgia pain

Tai chi, an ancient Chinese practice of exercise and meditation, may relieve symptoms of a painful chronic condition called fibromyalgia, a new study shows.

Tai chi involves gentle, flowing movements in which students shift their weight and breathe deeply, cycling through a series of [poses] with poetic names, such as "white crane spreads its wings."

The philosophy of tai chi involves moving a person's vital energy, or *qi* ("chee"), through the body.

In the study, doctors randomly assigned 66 fibromyalgia patients to take either a 12-week tai chi class or attend a "wellness education" class that included stretching exercises, according to a study in today's *New England Journal of Medicine*.

USA TODAY Snapshots®

Yoga's followers

Nearly 16 million adults in the USA practice yoga. Practitioners by age:

18 to 34
41%

35 to 54
41%

over 55
18%

Source: *Yoga Journal* survey of 5,050 adults conducted by Harris Interactive.

By Michelle Healy and Veronica Salazar, USA TODAY, 2008

associated with yoga include muscle strain, as with any practice that challenges and stretches muscle groups. Most cities offer different types of yoga classes. Yoga DVDs are another way to learn more about yoga and to practice its techniques.

Fibromyalgia patients experience pain, stiffness, fatigue and other problems.

All participants attended two hour-long classes a week and had instructions to practice at home 20 minutes a day. Most were women with an average age of 50, and most were overweight.

After finishing the course, 79% of tai chi participants said their symptoms had improved, compared with 39% of those in the educational class. It was financed by the National Center for Complementary and Alternative Medicine, a branch of the National Institutes of Health.

Tai chi students reported improvements in mood, sleep, quality of life and their ability to exercise. Even three months after the classes ended, 82% of tai chi students still felt better, compared with 53% of the comparison group, the study says.

In an accompanying editorial, Harvard Medical School's Gloria Yeh and others note that the study had limitations. Yeh notes that researchers don't know which aspects of tai chi were most helpful: the exercise, deep breathing, relaxation exercise, meeting new friends or learning from a charismatic teacher.

Because all students knew which type of class they were taking, it's possible that tai chi could act like a placebo, so patients improved simply because they expected to.

Yeh suggests conducting a larger, longer study—with multiple teachers, at different locations, perhaps comparing it with yoga and other therapies—to really understand tai chi's benefits.

But tai chi has few drawbacks. Even the cost of a class is modest compared with the cost of many medications. And unlike drugs, tai chi had no harmful side effects.

—*Liz Szabo*

TAI CHI

Tai chi is a set of traditional Chinese physical postures developed about two thousand years ago. It is a series of slow, gentle movements combined with deep breathing and meditation. Health professionals recommend tai chi for reducing stress and increasing balance and flexibility. Tai chi involves very little risk. In fact, many older adults practice tai chi to reduce the chances of falling. Practicing tai chi can help people at any age or fitness level to increase stamina and agility. Tai chi is usually practiced in group classes. An instructor leads the class through a series of slow, graceful movements, one leading into the next without pausing. Once you have learned the postures, you can practice tai chi anywhere at any time.

CHAPTER FOUR

HANDS-ON TREATMENTS

REX'S STORY

Rex, a seven-year-old Akita, had always been a graceful dog. He loved romping happily around the farm where he lived and effortlessly keeping his owner's livestock in line. But as Rex got older, he showed signs of discomfort in his hindquarters. One summer day, he began to limp as he made his way through the pasture. Tim, Rex's owner, wondered what was wrong.

Tim took Rex to his regular vet to find out what the problem might be. After X-rays and other tests, the vet diagnosed Rex with canine hip dysplasia. This disease of the hip joint can be very painful. The disease cannot be cured, so vets focus on finding ways to lessen discomfort. Surgery and medications can help, but there are risks and side effects. Tim was unhappy with these options, so the vet suggested alternative therapy for Rex.

The next day, Tim took Rex to Dr. Cathy, a vet who specializes in alternative medicine for companion animals. After evaluating Rex and reviewing the other vet's notes, Dr. Cathy and Tim agreed to a four-part course of treatment for Rex at her clinic. The treatment would involve chiropractic sessions, physical therapy, acupuncture, and nutritional therapy.

Tim followed Dr. Cathy's advice, and Rex's symptoms eased. He was not able to run through the pasture with the same energy and freedom as he had when he was a puppy. But the limp was much less obvious, and he suffered less pain. He lived many more years and did not have to deal with the sometimes debilitating side effects of surgery and traditional medications.

Part of Rex's treatment program involved hands-on therapy. These treatments can bring about physical and emotional healing in animals like Rex as well as in humans. Hands-on therapies include chiropractic and osteopathic adjustments, massage, the Alexander Technique, rolfing, and reflexology.

CHIROPRACTIC ADJUSTMENTS

Chiropractic medicine involves the manipulation of the spine and other parts of the body. The goals are to lessen pain and restore proper nerve function. The ancient Greeks practiced spinal manipulation. Twenty-first century chiropractic practice has existed for only about a hundred years. Some chiropractors believe that chiropractic treatments can keep away and even cure disease. While there is no scientific proof of this, chiropractic sessions can relieve low back pain, headaches, and other spine-related conditions.

In 1980 the American Medical Association accepted the chiropractic method as a proven treatment. A 1994 study by the U.S. Department of Health and Human Services concluded that spinal manipulation is effective in relieving severe low back pain. It can have better results than

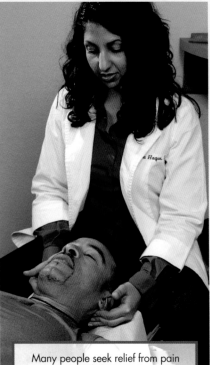

Many people seek relief from pain and discomfort through chiropractic treatment. Always check to make sure your chiropractor is licensed.

surgery, medication, and other conventional treatments. For this reason, many insurance companies will pay for a certain number of chiropractic sessions every year.

To adjust the spine, a chiropractor uses his or her hands to apply a sudden force to a joint to try to improve its range of motion. He or she may also use massage to relax muscles. The chiropractor may also choose to stimulate muscles with an electrical charge. In general, five or six sessions may be effective in treating low back pain.

Manipulation of the neck can lead to injury. As with other types of alternative therapy, be sure to check that your chiropractor is licensed in your state.

OSTEOPATHY

Osteopathy is a form of whole-body (mind, body, and spirit) medicine that focuses on treating and strengthening the body's muscular and skeletal framework. Its goal is to positively impact the body's nervous, circulatory, and lymphatic systems without the use of drugs or surgery. Osteopaths use hands-on techniques to balance all body systems, not just the area that is causing pain or other health problems.

After the deaths of his three children in 1864 from spinal meningitis, an American physician and surgeon—Dr. Andrew Taylor Still—began looking for new ways to treat disease. He was one of the first doctors in the United States to study the causes of disease (rather than focusing only on treating symptoms). Additionally, he believed in looking for ways to maintain good health as a way to avoid illness in the first place. In the twenty-first century, this approach to health is called preventive medicine. In 1892 Dr. Still founded the world's first school of osteopathy—the American School of Osteopathy—in Missouri.

In broad terms, osteopathic treatment is believed to work by using the body's own forces to do the job of healing. By applying gentle forces in a very precise way, osteopaths try to release the body's strains and its patterns of trauma and stress. In your first session with an osteopath, you can expect to discuss your health situation with the practitioner. He or she will then do gentle hands-on adjustments or manipulations of joints and bones. Doctors of osteopathic medicine (DOs) are highly trained professionals. With the appropriate degree, training, and licensure, DOs can legally practice medicine and perform surgeries in all fifty states. To find a reputable osteopath in your area, start by searching the American Osteopathic Association website at http://www.osteopathic.org.

MASSAGE

Massage is more than a spa treatment. Therapeutic massage is the manipulation of soft tissue (muscles, skin, and tendons) by a trained practitioner. Massage is recommended by health practitioners to relieve stress, reduce muscle soreness, and help patients to relax.

It has many benefits, such as increasing blood flow to the muscles,

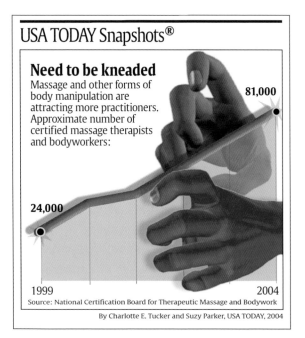

USA TODAY Snapshots®

Need to be kneaded
Massage and other forms of body manipulation are attracting more practitioners. Approximate number of certified massage therapists and bodyworkers:

81,000

24,000

1999   2004

Source: National Certification Board for Therapeutic Massage and Bodywork

By Charlotte E. Tucker and Suzy Parker, USA TODAY, 2004

September 29, 2008

From the Pages of USA TODAY

Human touch may have some healing properties

It can lower stress and blood pressure

A new study from researchers in Utah finds that a warm touch—the nonsexual, supportive kind—[helps reduce] stress and blood pressure, adding to a growing body of research on how emotions affect health.

The study of 34 young married couples ages 20 to 39 by researchers at Brigham Young University in Provo [Utah] and the University of Utah in Salt Lake City found that massage and other supportive and caring touch lower stress hormones and blood pressure, particularly among men, while also enhancing oxytocin, a hormone thought to calm and counter stress. The findings will be published in the Oct. 14 issue of the journal *Psychosomatic Medicine*.

Brigham Young psychology professor Julianne Holt-Lunstad says the study aimed to learn whether increasing the level of supportive physical contact would improve health-related physical outcomes.

Twenty couples, all married at least six months, participated in a four-week [course] that promoted emotional and physical closeness. They were brought into the lab for training and testing, but the bulk of their actions were at home, including a 30-minute massage (neck, shoulder or forehead) three times a week. Participants wore portable blood pressure monitors for 24 hours to supply a number

relieving pain and discomfort, and creating a sense of general well-being. Massage is generally safe. However, if it is done incorrectly, it can cause pain and even injury.

Be sure to ask your massage therapist about his or her training and qualifications. If you live in a state that requires therapists to have licenses, make sure that your therapist has one. And if something of readings. They also completed questionnaires about how often they hugged, kissed, held hands or were otherwise affectionate. The 14-couple control group had testing but not the [course].

"While a fair amount has been done on massage's effects on anxiety and depression and seems to have a positive impact, we don't know that much about specific biological factors," says Gail Ironson, a physician and professor of psychology and psychiatry at the University of Miami in Coral Gables, Florida.

Behavioral neurobiologist C. Sue Carter of the University of Illinois at Chicago says taking the study out of the laboratory is [unique] because such settings may increase stress.

"The nice thing about this study is that it lets people live in their own world and see effects of their own social interactions without the complexities" of being in a lab, she says.

"If it can help couples who are already young and healthy, it may have a greater effect among older couples or couples with health problems," she says. "Certainly, being more affectionate with your spouse wouldn't hurt."

—Sharon Jayson

Taking time to quickly massage your partner a few times a week can mean lower stress levels and blood pressure.

hurts during a massage session, speak up! Too much pressure can cause internal bleeding and nerve damage.

OTHER HANDS-ON THERAPIES

Other hands-on therapies include the Alexander Technique, rolfing, and reflexology. These approaches are not generally accepted by the medical community and carry greater risk than massage and spinal manipulation. Legal requirements for practicing these therapies vary widely, so proceed with caution if you choose to seek any of these treatments.

ALEXANDER TECHNIQUE

Frederick Matthias Alexander (1869–1955) was an Australian actor who developed problems with hoarseness that his doctor could not explain or cure. To treat himself, Alexander developed a technique based on the link he observed between posture, body movement, breathing and physical pain, breathing problems, and physical tension. People who use this technique do so to try to relieve pain, prevent injury, and improve general body function. A teacher of the Alexander Technique orally coaches a group of students on how to relax the neck, improve posture, and undo unhealthy habits of the body such as slouching. The teacher also uses gentle hands-on corrections to show students how to make adjustments to posture, movement, and breathing. Its effectiveness has not been proven through clinical research.

ROLFING

Rolfing is a nickname for Rolfing Structural Integration (Rolfing SI). This form of bodywork was developed by Dr. Ida P. Rolf (1896–1979). She received her Ph.D. in biochemistry from Columbia University in New York in 1920. To treat her own health problems, she explored a variety of alternative treatments over many years. She concluded that manipulating the body's connective tissues (muscles, fascia, tendons, and ligaments) leads to better posture and more freedom of movement. Practitioners of Rolfing SI use their fingers, knuckles, thumbs, elbows, and knees to manipulate tissues and muscles.

Some people find Rolfing SI sessions to be painful. And while it can help lessen low back pain and improve posture, flexibility, and balance, Rolfing SI can cause injury. Pregnant women, people with osteoporosis or rheumatoid arthritis, or anyone taking medications to thin the blood should not use Rolfing SI.

REFLEXOLOGY

In this therapy, a reflexologist uses thumb, finger, and hand techniques to apply pressure to points on the feet and hands. This pressure can relieve stress and pain and improve blood flow in the body. Reflexology is an ancient practice, with roots in Egypt, China, and Japan. Reflexologists believe that certain areas on the soles of the feet and on the hands correspond to other parts of the body. Reflexologists use charts of the feet and hands to pinpoint their work. Based on the charts, they apply pressure to certain points to help relieve symptoms elsewhere in the body. Scientific evidence does not prove the effectiveness of this treatment. Nonetheless, a good foot or hand massage involves very little risk.

CHAPTER FIVE

ENERGY-BASED THERAPY

JASON'S STORY

After Jason was nearly killed in a motorcycle accident, he faced a long series of surgeries to repair fractures in his spine, pelvis, shoulder, and thigh. He did not tolerate surgical anesthesia well. After each operation, he felt disoriented and nauseous for several days.

Jason's family helped him research methods for lessening the side effects of the anesthesia. One day, his sister came across an article on acupuncture. The article said that the National Institutes of Health (NIH) had endorsed acupuncture as an effective treatment for some kinds of nausea. This included nausea associated with surgical anesthesia. The article also recommended acupuncture for combating pain from dental surgery.

Jason talked to his doctor about acupuncture. They discussed the history of the procedure and reviewed the NIH panel's conclusions together. They both agreed that acupuncture was worth a try.

Jason consulted with a licensed acupuncturist named Julie. She thoroughly reviewed Jason's medical history. After Jason's next surgery, Julie inserted about a dozen slender needles into specific points in Jason's skin, moving them gently into place. Julie left the needles in for about thirty minutes. During this time, Jason relaxed in his softly lit hospital room, where Julie had put on soft, calming music. After the thirty minutes were up, she came back into Jason's room and quickly removed the needles, leaving no traces.

When Jason was fully awake, he was pleased that he felt no nausea from the anesthesia. During the next several days, Jason had several more acupuncture treatments to relieve pain from the surgery. He felt only a slight sensation when Julie inserted the needles.

"I've never been through an operation with so little nausea and pain," he said. "I'm not sure how acupuncture works, but it seems to have helped me."

SIMON'S STORY

Simon had studied the violin since he was six years old. By the time he was ten, he was performing with adults in a local symphony orchestra. When he was fifteen, Simon won a national violin competition. At the age of twenty-four, he was concertmaster of a metropolitan symphony orchestra.

But when he was thirty-three, all of Simon's success came crashing down. A vague feeling of discomfort in his right wrist grew quickly into sharp pain along his entire forearm. The pain was accompanied by muscular weakness in his hand. The pain and weakness made it difficult for Simon to hold his violin bow. He also had trouble gliding it masterfully over the strings of his violin as he had for so many years.

Simon's doctor diagnosed him with carpal tunnel syndrome. This syndrome involves compression of nerves in the wrist. It causes pain, numbness, and weakness. The physician prescribed a program of rest, exercises, anti-inflammatory drugs, and painkillers. Simon felt little relief from the treatment, however. And the drugs had side effects, including drowsiness. Since Simon could not play his violin regularly, he had to take a break from his musical career.

After a few months, Simon's doctor suggested that surgery might be an option. Simon was desperate to get back to his musical career. But he was worried about an operation that might cause him to lose permanent control in his right hand. He decided to investigate alternative treatments that would not be so invasive.

After informing his doctor of his plans, Simon went to work. First, he visited a specialist in acupressure. This treatment is similar to acupuncture but does not require needles.

The acupressure specialist taught Simon how to apply pressure to a point near his right wrist. The specialist told Simon to repeat the exercise at home three times a day. Simon also learned about other acupressure treatments, including ones thought to relieve stress and insomnia. Simon was eager to try, since these were problems he was struggling with because of the break in his music career.

In addition, Simon saw a nutritionist. She said that dietary changes could help him heal. For example, sugar, caffeine, and processed grains can cause a deficiency in vitamin B_6, she told Simon. This vitamin shortage is common among people who suffer from carpal tunnel syndrome. She recommended that Simon cut back on sugar and caffeine. She also suggested that he increase his intake of foods rich in vitamin B_6, including whole grains and fish.

In addition, Simon decided to visit an herbalist. They talked about Simon's carpal tunnel syndrome, and the herbalist gave Simon a mixture of anti-inflammatory herbs.

The alternative treatments didn't work. The pain in Simon's wrist decreased for a while. But when he began practicing regularly again, the numbness, pain, and loss of control returned.

Eventually, Simon decided to have the surgery for his carpal tunnel condition. The surgery went well, and he recovered quickly. Soon, Simon was back at work, playing violin with the symphony orchestra. In Simon's case, conventional Western medicine—not alternative therapy—addressed Simon's problem. Even so, Simon continued to follow some of the dietary and acupressure measures he had learned. He believed they helped him remain healthy long after his carpal tunnel problem was cured.

People who practice energy-based therapies believe that imbalance in the body's energy results in illness or pain. Acupuncture, acupressure, therapeutic touch, and Reiki are among the methods that some claim can activate the body's natural energy and restore energy that is weak or out of balance.

ACUPUNCTURE

Acupuncture originated in China thousands of years ago and has become very popular in the United States since the 1970s. In 2007 the National Health Interview Survey estimated that 3.1 million U.S. adults used acupuncture. The method can be an effective treatment for the following:

- Headaches
- Nausea and vomiting
- Pain management, including dental pain and labor pains during childbirth
- Osteoarthritis
- Side effects of chemotherapy

According to traditional Chinese medicine, illness is caused by an imbalance in the body's energy. This imbalance leads to blockages in the flow of chi (vital energy) along pathways known as meridians. To restore balance and free up this energy, an acupuncturist

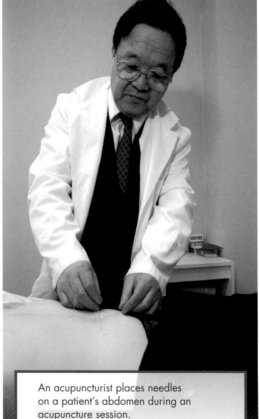

An acupuncturist places needles on a patient's abdomen during an acupuncture session.

places thin, sterilized, stainless steel needles at various depths at points on the body that are connected to the meridians. Acupuncture was not well known in the United States until the early 1970s. At that time, U.S. journalist James Reston had emergency surgery in China. He received nothing but acupuncture to manage the postoperative pain. Reston wrote about his experience, and many Americans then became interested in the procedure. Since then, acupuncture has

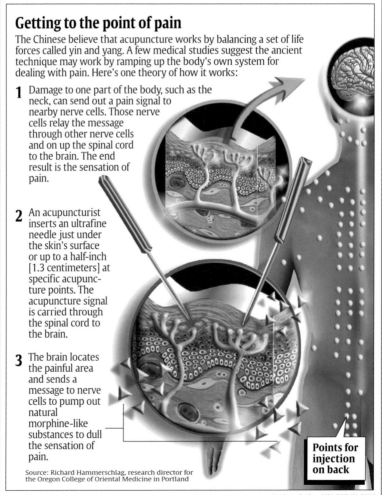

Getting to the point of pain

The Chinese believe that acupuncture works by balancing a set of life forces called yin and yang. A few medical studies suggest the ancient technique may work by ramping up the body's own system for dealing with pain. Here's one theory of how it works:

1 Damage to one part of the body, such as the neck, can send out a pain signal to nearby nerve cells. Those nerve cells relay the message through other nerve cells and on up the spinal cord to the brain. The end result is the sensation of pain.

2 An acupuncturist inserts an ultrafine needle just under the skin's surface or up to a half-inch [1.3 centimeters] at specific acupuncture points. The acupuncture signal is carried through the spinal cord to the brain.

3 The brain locates the painful area and sends a message to nerve cells to pump out natural morphine-like substances to dull the sensation of pain.

Source: Richard Hammerschlag, research director for the Oregon College of Oriental Medicine in Portland

Points for injection on back

By Suzy Parker, USA TODAY, 2005

become one of the most widely embraced alternative treatments in the United States. According to some surveys, as many as 15 million Americans have tried acupuncture at least once. And many insurance programs pay for acupuncture sessions related to pain management.

In the West, researchers tend to doubt theories about meridians and invisible energy flow. Some speculate that acupuncture works by releasing such substances as endorphins, which are chemicals in the brain that can reduce pain. Other researchers believe that acupuncture subtly affects nerve pathways in the body, blocking sensations of pain. Relatively few Western physicians view acupuncture as a viable replacement for surgical anesthesia. But it is gaining acceptance as a complementary treatment.

While much is still unknown about acupuncture, the NIH has concluded that it is safe. It is relatively free of side effects when done properly. And however it may work, acupuncture's promise as a therapeutic tool has come through for many Americans.

ACUPRESSURE

Like acupuncture, acupressure is built on the ancient Asian concept of chi. Using fingers or thumbs, the practitioner applies strong pressure at key points on the body. The pressure is applied downward or in line with the flow of the energy channel. In this way, some people believe that acupressure rebalances a person's chi and allows it to flow freely. They believe it helps to restore health to the region of the body that is suffering.

Many Western researchers doubt the existence of chi. They think of acupressure as a form of deep massage that stimulates blood flow to an affected area. It may create electrical impulses or release chemicals in the body that block pain and aid healing.

February 22, 2010

From the Pages of USA TODAY

Healing is name of game
Athletes willingly try new methods

Downhill skiers are known as a daring lot, and even more so practitioners of the new Olympic sport called ski cross, so it might come as no surprise some would turn to innovative medical treatments to accelerate their recovery from injuries.

American skiers Casey Puckett and Daron Rahlves made it back from recent severe injuries to compete Sunday in the Vancouver [Olympic] Games, though neither reached the medal round.

Experts on the field say the pursuit of cutting-edge treatments for injuries is common among Olympic and pro athletes in all disciplines who make a living with their bodies and have plenty to lose by extended absences from the arena.

Puckett overcame a Jan. 10 shoulder dislocation that required surgery with a combination of physical therapy, acupuncture and time in a hyperbaric chamber. Rahlves raced three weeks after dislocating a hip, thanks to sessions of physical therapy, magnetic pulse therapy, acupuncture and treatment with platelet-rich plasma (PRP).

Other elite athletes are sure to [notice].

The menu of treatment options for sports injuries has never been richer, as old staples such as anterior cruciate ligament and Tommy John surgeries have been joined by new alternatives such as PRP, minimally invasive sports hernia surgery, low-intensity laser therapy and prolotherapy.

In addition, researchers at the Steadman Philippon Research Institute in Vail, Colorado, recently have concluded a study on the effects of stem cells on cartilage regeneration, and New York surgeon David Altchek, the New York Mets' medical director, reports encouraging results in a new procedure to repair rotator cuff tears in pitchers.

On the public radar

Avoiding the operating room is a strong motivator for athletes who have tried PRP, a procedure that involves taking a small syringe of blood from a patient's body, spinning it in a centrifuge to isolate the platelets—which act as healing agents—and injecting about a teaspoon of the richer plasma into the injured area.

The treatment is approved by the World Anti-Doping Agency as long as the injections are not applied to the muscles, because that could promote their growth.

Allan Mishra, an orthopedic surgeon in Northern California who pioneered the use of PRP, says the therapy has shown promising results in treating patients with acute tendinitis in the elbow and knee.

PRP drew national attention last year when Pittsburgh Steelers wide receiver Hines Ward used it to speed his recovery from a sprained knee ligament before the Super Bowl. Even PRP's skeptics acknowledge the treatment is safe—some believe it's overhyped or doubt its effectiveness—and Mishra says researchers are trying to figure out the ideal formulation, concentration and use of it. An article in the *American Journal of Sports Medicine* this month detailed a study that found PRP significantly more effective than cortisone for tennis elbow.

New York Giants defensive tackle Chris Canty says he didn't know much about PRP when team trainers suggested he try it for a stubborn hamstring injury last preseason. Canty was so pleased with the results that he used PRP again later in the season when he had an injured calf.

"You can kind of call me the spokesperson for the PRP procedure in our locker room," Canty says. "I tell guys that are having problems with tendinitis or problems with tears in muscles that it's painful, but it is well worth it, and you start feeling better within days, not weeks."

A year after his 15-year career as an NFL quarterback ended in 1999, Steve Bono tore his left Achilles tendon playing basketball and had it operated on by Mishra. About six weeks later, Bono heard about PRP from former San Francisco 49ers teammate Joe Montana, who owned horses and learned veterinarians used the technique on them.

Mishra did research. When Bono tore his other Achilles a year and a half later—playing basketball again—they made PRP part of the repair, even though the procedure was in its infancy.

"Athletes are very willing to go to great lengths and try innovative techniques and treatments," says Bono, who recovered in six months, two to three months faster than the first Achilles surgery.

Looking for help

Oakland Athletics third baseman Eric Chavez doesn't expect to return to his 100%, Gold Glove-winning days. He'll settle for getting on the field regularly.

Chavez, who has played in 121 of a possible 485 games in the last three seasons because of back and shoulder woes, spent more than $10,000 each on two machines meant to stimulate blood flow to his injuries and help them heal.

The latest machine, which emits a red laser light, comes on the heels of trying acupuncture, chiropractors and massage therapists.

Chavez says the machines provide relief from pain but don't address its source. Then again, he has had surgeries on both shoulders and two back operations since 2007, without the desired results.

Therefore, like so many athletes seeking a return to action, he's willing to experiment.

—*Jorge L. Ortiz*

A woman undergoes an acupressure treatment focusing on points on her face.

Still, conventional healers have not ruled out the possible benefits of acupressure. Clinical studies have supported the usefulness of some strategic acupressure points. For example, scientific research supports the use of acupressure applied to the wrist to relieve nausea related to anesthesia used during surgery. It also may help lessen morning sickness during pregnancy as well as motion sickness.

THERAPEUTIC TOUCH

Therapeutic touch comes from ancient healing practices in Asian and American Indian cultures. In modern times, it was developed in the early 1970s by Dr. Dolores Krieger, a nursing professor at New York University, and Dora Kunz, a healer. People who support therapeutic touch believe the human body has energy fields that a trained practitioner can feel. If the flow of energy in these fields is blocked, disease can result. A therapist seeks to locate and correct any blockages in these energy fields.

In a therapeutic touch session, the practitioner first scans the person's body from head to toe. The therapist does this by passing his or her hands 2 to 4 inches (5 to 10 cm) above the skin. The therapist then touches the person at key points on the body. Some

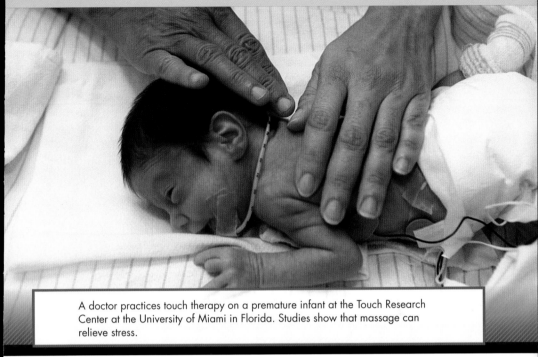

A doctor practices touch therapy on a premature infant at the Touch Research Center at the University of Miami in Florida. Studies show that massage can relieve stress.

claim this moves energy through the therapist to the person and is meant to boost self-healing.

Therapeutic touch is taught to nursing students around the world. Many people feel that therapeutic touch can relieve pain, ease stress, treat some diseases, and soothe crying babies. Research into the effectiveness of therapeutic touch is ongoing. Most conventional health-care professionals do not prescribe therapeutic touch as a cure for disease. However, there is little to no risk associated with this method. For this reason, conventional doctors generally will not discourage their patients from trying it.

REIKI

The term *Reiki* (RAY-kee) comes from the Japanese words *rei*, or "universal spirit," and *qi*, meaning "life force energy." Reiki is based on the same principles as other forms of energy-based therapy. People who practice Reiki healing feel it can ease side effects, reduce

Emily Rosa Takes On Therapeutic Touch

Some medical professionals have always viewed therapeutic touch with deep suspicion. A research study published in the *Journal of the American Medical Association* in the late 1990s challenged the claims of Dr. Krieger and her supporters.

The study was designed and conducted by a grade-school student named Emily Rosa of Loveland, Colorado. The research report on the study was prepared by Emily's mother, Linda, a nurse and critic of touch therapy; Larry Sarner of the National Therapeutic Touch Study Group, which questions the approach; and Dr. Stephen Barrett of Quackwatch, a nonprofit group that posts information on the Internet about controversial medical practices. Emily tested the claims of therapeutic touch in a fourth-grade science fair experiment.

Twenty-one therapeutic-touch practitioners took part in the experiment. They had experience in the technique ranging from one to twenty-seven years. Emily tested them to find out whether they could determine which of their hands was closest to her own hand by sensing its energy field. Emily placed her hand over either the right or left hand of a practitioner, letting it hover there. Placement of her hand was decided by flipping a

stress and anxiety, and even cure any disease or health condition. Clinical research supports its use only for stress relief and relaxation.

In a Reiki session, you can expect to remain fully clothed. You will be asked to either lie down on a massage table or sit in a chair. The Reiki therapist places his or her hands on or near the body, using coin. A tall screen prevented the practitioners from seeing where Emily was placing her hand.

The practitioners identified the correct hand in only 44 percent of 280 trials. This is close to the rate that would be expected by random chance. To prove touch therapy's validity, the study's authors said that the practitioners should have been able to find Emily's hand 100 percent of the time. The fact that they couldn't shows that therapeutic touch should not be used professionally.

In a news report of the study, supporters of therapeutic touch defended the practice and said the experiment was not valid. Dr. Krieger herself says that the technique works. She went on to say that Emily Rosa did not understand how to do basic research.

But in a note attached to the study, Dr. George D. Lundberg, the editor of the journal, said the experiment was indeed valid. He felt that practitioners of therapeutic touch should tell their patients about the study so they can decide if they want to proceed with the treatment.

Lundberg also included a useful comment about the entire field of unconventional therapy. He noted that Americans are interested in alternative therapies, some of which have been proven to work and some of which haven't.

specific Reiki hand positions. The therapist holds the position for two to five minutes, until the therapist believes he or she feels the energy flow from practitioner to recipient slow or stop. Then the therapist moves to the next area on the body. A session generally lasts between thirty and ninety minutes.

September 15, 2008

From the Pages of USA TODAY

Alternative treatments serve mind, body, spirit

Unconventional therapies enhance patients' hospital experience, healing

When nurses tried to insert an IV [needle] into patient Linda Aron's hand, she was so anxious over the [upcoming] operation to fix her acid reflux that they simply had to stop.

Instead of continuing to poke and prod Aron, nurses at Grinnell (Iowa) Regional Medical Center called in a massage therapist to rub her shoulders and arms to help her relax. Within 10 minutes, Aron had an IV in place.

To meet patient demand and [improve] the hospital experience, more hospitals like Grinnell offer patients complementary and alternative treatments. The American Hospital Association (AHA) says that 37% of hospitals around the USA make complementary and alternative treatments available—including acupuncture, touch therapy, and music and art therapy.

A similar survey by the hospital group in 2005 found that one in four hospitals offered such services.

Patients such as Aron say they are surprised at how some of these therapies make a difference in their hospital experience.

"It was wonderful to have someone take your mind off of what was going on," Aron says. "Having the human touch and knowing that someone is paying very personal attention to you helps. It keeps everything from being so medical."

And, to help speed her recovery and relieve pain from the surgery, Aron currently receives weekly acupuncture from the hospital in Grinnell as an outpatient. She pays the $55 fee out of her own pocket.

"This is a movement toward 'patient-centered' care," says Sita Ananth, director of knowledge services for the Samueli Institute, an Alexandria, Virginia-based non-profit that studies alternative therapies. "Many hospital mission statements are to serve the mind, body and spiritual needs of their patients."

Success measured in patient satisfaction

While these types of therapies have a useful place in the hospital, more data are needed to understand how they work, says Andrew Schafer, chief physician at New York-Presbyterian Hospital/Weill Cornell Medical Center. "Complementary and alternative therapies must be [examined] in terms of their risk-to-benefit ratio and be subjected to placebo-controlled studies.

"If it turns out that the placebo effect is at work, that is not necessarily a bad thing," he adds, "but today's complementary and alternative therapies could be tomorrow's medical breakthroughs."

The majority of hospitals say that patient satisfaction is the No. 1 way they determine if an alternative treatment is beneficial, closely followed by clinical data on a treatment. Cleveland Clinic [in Ohio] just completed a complementary and alternative therapy pilot program for patients undergoing heart surgery. Half of the patients—more than 1,700—opted for spiritual care, counseling, art, music, touch therapy or guided imagery, and 93% of patients surveyed said the services were helpful.

Guidance from doctor groups for patients with chronic pain has helped bolster doctors' acceptance of complementary treatments, says Richard Nahin, senior adviser for scientific coordination and outreach at the National Center for Complementary and Alternative Medicine. He cites new guidelines for treating lower back pain issued jointly last year by the American College of Physicians and the American Pain Society, which suggest many alternative therapies as potential treatments. "As doctors become more aware, hospitals will also follow," Nahin says.

Not all doctors are on board

Yet the picture is not so rosy at certain centers. According to the AHA, 44% of hospitals that offer such therapies say that their programs have a mediocre or poor relationship with staff physicians.

Betty Carlson, 79, of Fenton, Michigan, doesn't need to be sold on the benefits. She received regular sessions with a Reiki therapist, a form of spiritual healing, and a spiritual adviser during her month-long stay at Cleveland Clinic after open heart surgery. As a retired nursing home administrator, Carlson says she was skeptical when first introduced to Reiki by a friend, but she quickly discovered how it helped relieve pain.

"It was very relaxing, and a gift toward my healing."

—*Lisa Gill*

CHAPTER SIX

WHOLE MEDICAL SYSTEMS

IRENE'S STORY

A retired dance teacher, Irene loved to do the challenging New York Times crossword puzzle every day. She also loved reading and read two books a week. She read everything from mysteries to nonfiction works on science and history. Yet as mentally alert as she was, Irene suffered from high blood pressure, aching and stiff joints, and chronic fatigue. Once an active gardener, she had given it up because of her physical problems. The small patch of earth outside her bedroom window lay untended and choked with weeds.

One day, looking through a book on Chinese medicine, Irene found a chapter on qigong (pronounced "chee gong"). A tradition that is thousands of years old, medical qigong combines physical and breathing exercises with meditation. Irene read that tens of millions of people in China practice qigong. She learned that it can be a very useful therapy for many health problems, including high blood pressure and arthritis. Irene decided to give it a try.

Irene learned of a qigong group that was set to begin classes at her city's community center. From her very first class, she could see benefits to qigong. She liked its emphasis on breathing, movement, mental focusing, and relaxation.

Irene enjoyed her qigong classes. Her teacher did not force her to do exercises she did not feel physically prepared for. She felt safe in class. Soon she was able to practice qigong on her own. She felt energized by the exercises and experienced improvements in her blood pressure. Her joints also became less stiff. When spring came, Irene began planting flowers again.

The history of whole medical systems lies in many different cultures. These systems focus on physical, mental, and spiritual health. Like most practitioners of CAM, people who practice within a system of whole medicine believe that the mind and the body must both be involved in well-being. They believe that the body has the ability to heal itself. Practitioners focus on prevention of illness and on keeping the body in balance. They recommend plans for nutrition, exercise, sleep, and daily routines that promote good health. These practices differ from conventional Western medicine in that treatments are individualized. No two people will receive exactly the same "prescription" from a practitioner.

Western systems of whole medicine include homeopathy, naturopathy, and osteopathy. The two most widely practiced Eastern systems are traditional Chinese medicine (TCM) and Ayurveda, which comes originally from India.

HOMEOPATHY

The term *homeopathy* comes from the Greek words *homeo*, which means "similar," and *pathos*, meaning "suffering" or "disease." German physician Samuel Hahnemann developed this medical system in the 1790s. In Hahnemann's time, standard medical practices of the day included bleeding patients. In the process of bloodletting, doctors rid the body of blood, sometimes using leeches to suck out the blood. They bled patients, believing they were balancing the body's "humors" when they felt these forces were out of balance. Doctors also prescribed dangerous toxins (poisons), such as mercury, to cure diseases such as syphilis. Hahnemann felt that these treatments did more harm than healing, and he began to look for alternative treatments.

Homeopathy is based on the theory that small amounts of a

medicine will treat a disease even though that same substance would produce symptoms of the disease in a healthy person who takes larger doses. Two other main ideas guide homeopathy. One is that homeopathic medicines become more effective as they are diluted (weakened in strength). The second is that a single medicine can treat all symptoms, both physical and mental. This is a very different approach from conventional treatment, which often uses separate medicines for each symptom.

Hahnemann's method has two main principles: the principle of similars and the principle of dilutions.

- **Similars (or "like cures like").** The idea of similars rests on the belief that a disease can be cured by a substance that produces symptoms of the disease in healthy people. Hahnemann had read about cinchona bark, a natural treatment for malaria. He tried an experiment in which he drank a liquid version of the bark twice a day for a few days. He found that he developed the symptoms of malaria. From that experience, Hahnemann concluded that if a substance caused disease symptoms in a healthy person, small amounts could, in turn, cure a person of the disease.

- **Dilutions (or "law of minimum dose").** The idea of dilutions rests on the belief that low doses of medication are more effective than high doses. Homeopathic remedies are natural substances that are diluted (usually in water, sugar, or alcohol). This process is called potentization. A trained homeopath places the substance in the dilutant (liquid) and shakes it vigorously. This is repeated a number of times, using less of the substance each time. Through this process, properties of the substance move naturally to the dilutant. The final product contains very little and sometimes none of the healing substance. Homeopaths believe that the diluted substance leaves an imprint—its essence—in the dilutant.

This homeopathic pharmacist measures a dose of an herbal mixture. Homeopathic remedies are made of natural substances that are diluted.

When the patient takes the medicine, it stimulates the body to heal itself.

At the beginning of the 1900s, 15 percent of U.S. physicians were homeopaths. As medical science advanced throughout the century, homeopathy lost its popularity. But as Americans began gaining interest in alternative medicine in the 1970s, new attention has been focused on homeopathy in the United States.

DOES IT WORK?

There is debate among scientists and doctors as to whether homeopathic treatments work. Some claim that homeopathy offers an effective alternative to antibiotics. They say it is often the best approach for treating viral infections. Homeopathy can also help patients avoid some surgeries, they say. Nonetheless, homeopathic practitioners do recommend conventional treatments in cases of severe sickness.

Critics of homeopathic medicine say that many clinical studies of homeopathy have been scientifically flawed. They also point to product labels on homeopathic products that lack enough information to judge dosages. And they say that some homeopathic remedies have proved to be harmful. What's more, critics say that the Food and Drug Administration, which regulates homeopathic remedies, has not held them to the same standards as other drugs.

NATUROPATHY

Naturopathy is a whole medical system based on the belief that the body can heal itself. One of the key founders of naturopathy was Benedict Lust (1872–1945), a German waiter. He used a popular water cure to treat himself for what he thought was tuberculosis. After that experience with natural healing, he opened the world's first medical school of naturopathy—the American School of Naturopathy—in New York in the early 1900s.

As with other types of holistic healing, the main philosophy of naturopathic medicine is that the body has the power to heal itself. Naturopaths work to find and remove the causes of illness rather than to treat only the symptoms. Naturopathic professionals also work with patients to help each person promote his or her own health.

In a first session with a naturopath, that person will interview the patient to learn about his or her lifestyle, medical history, and emotional life. The naturopath will also do a physical exam. To help the individual patient maintain wellness, the naturopath may recommend acupuncture, herbs, and other forms of traditional

Chinese medicine; color therapy; exposure to sun and fresh air; changes in diet; meditation; reflexology; talk therapy, and other options.

Naturopaths have a variety of training. For example, naturopathic medical colleges in the United States and Canada offer extensive training. However, regulation of naturopathic medicine varies from state to state. If you decide to meet with a naturopath, check with an organization such as the American Association of Naturopathic Physicians. This organization offers more information about naturopathy and can help you find a certified naturopath in your area.

TRADITIONAL CHINESE MEDICINE

Traditional Chinese medicine dates back about five thousand years. In China, TCM is still practiced alongside Western medicine in many hospitals and clinics. Since the 1970s, many Americans have come to accept TCM, particularly acupuncture (which is also an energy-based therapy). Other treatments include Chinese herbs, dietary guidelines, massage, therapeutic exercise and movement (tai chi), and qigong.

TCM is based on the belief that good health comes from a balance of two forces: yin and yang. In simple terms, yin represents darkness and cold. Yang represents light and heat. An imbalance of these two forces causes a blockage in the flow of vital life energy (qi, or chi), TCM practitioners believe. The goal of TCM treatments is to unblock the body's energy pathways and restore health.

QIGONG

A therapy for fitness and healing, qigong has elements of meditation, movement, relaxation, and breathing exercises and techniques.

Qigong requires daily practice. The goal, practitioners say, is to build up the body's flow of chi and direct it to specific spots to improve health and to promote healing.

A controversial aspect of qigong is known as external healing. Some people claim that qigong masters can actually direct their vital energy toward another person. The claim is that directed energy helps in healing through powers, though such powers are not proven scientifically.

As Irene's qigong instructor explained, the basic techniques of qigong can help reduce blood pressure, improve the delivery of oxygen to the body's cells and tissues, and help with blood circulation. Among other things, it also can strengthen the body's immune system. To begin the practice, you can start slowly with just a few simple qigong exercises. You can also learn to use a set of qigong therapy balls that give off musical tones when rotated among the fingers. The exercise

A group practices qigong at a park in China. The mind-body practice of qigong dates back to ancient China.

is said to strengthen the tendons in the hand. It also massages what some believe to be the hand's energy points. This can help with blood circulation, muscle tone, and mental health.

AYURVEDA

The term *Ayurveda* comes from the Sanskrit words *ayus* (meaning "long life") and *veda* (meaning "related to knowledge" or "science"). Ayurvedic medicine was developed in India thousands of years ago. It is still practiced by most people in India, often along with conventional Western medicine. As with traditional Chinese medicine, more Americans have practiced Ayurveda since the 1970s.

Ayurvedic philosophy puts an equal emphasis on mind, body, and spirit. The goal is always to maintain or restore harmony and balance in the body. Practitioners of Ayurvedic medicine encourage people to eat, sleep, and take medicine in moderation. Bodily hygiene is also key to Ayurvedic medicine. Bathing and dental care are a key part of promoting well-being.

Some of the methods of Ayurvedic healing include fasting, breathing exercises, massage, meditation, and plant-based substances. In addition, practitioners prescribe sweating and steam-based therapies to open channels (*srotas*) that move the body's fluids from one point to another. Ayurvedic medicine believes that blocked channels can lead to a number of conditions, such as seizure disorders, paralysis, and mental health disturbances.

If you are interested in Ayurvedic medicine, remember that not all Ayurvedic practices are based on scientific research. In addition, the United States has no training or certification standards for the practice of Ayurvedic medicine. To learn more about Ayurveda, the National Center for Complementary and Alternative Medicine (http://nccam.nih.gov/health/ayurveda) is a good place to start.

January 8, 2007

From the Pages of USA TODAY

Tasty curry might have a fringe benefit; Research suggests turmeric may help prevent arthritis and a host of other diseases

Five years ago Darci Jayne hardly ever touched a vegetable and pretty much lived on pizza, pasta and fast food.

That diet led to weight gain and health problems, including severe joint pain. "I was close to 200 pounds [91 kg] and getting scared," she says.

By cutting portion sizes she lost 50 pounds [23 kg] but always felt as if she were on a diet. Then Jayne took an Indian cooking class that emphasized fresh vegetables and curry spices.

She began to whip up an Indian dinner once or twice a week — and soon she noticed she wasn't always looking for a late-night snack. And the curry in the food offered her a bonus: It seemed to ease the pain and swelling in her joints.

Preliminary research suggests Jayne may be right. A study in the November issue of *Arthritis & Rheumatism* suggests turmeric, one component of curry spice, almost completely prevented joint swelling in rats with arthritis. Other studies have suggested that the spice could protect against diseases such as heart disease,

cancer and Alzheimer's.

Rates of Alzheimer's in India are about four times lower than in the USA, says Gregory Cole, a researcher at the University of California-Los Angeles. His studies suggest that curry contains a powerful substance that might protect the brain from damage that leads to Alzheimer's.

Surprising findings in mice

Can scientists prove curry wards off such diseases as Alzheimer's or cancer? Not yet, says Bharat Aggarwal at the University of Texas-Houston. But he says the growing file on curry includes compelling evidence gleaned from animal and human studies.

The findings from Western science fit with what traditional Indian healers have long said about turmeric. "They call it the spice of life," says P. Murali Doraiswamy, an Alzheimer's expert at Duke University in Durham, N.C.

For centuries, doctors trained in Ayurvedic medicine, a traditional medical system in India, have turned to turmeric to treat inflammatory diseases such as arthritis, says Janet Funk, a researcher at the University of Kansas. In the USA, many people with arthritis take over-the-counter supplements that contain curcumin, the active ingredient in turmeric.

In the November study, Funk and her colleagues gave rats that were bred to develop rheumatoid arthritis injections of turmeric. "The turmeric almost completely prevented the onset of arthritis," Funk says. The spice also seemed to help stop joint destruction in rats that had already started to develop the disease, she says.

Curry also may offer some protection against cancer. "Indians eat [small amounts] of curry every day, and that might be enough to prevent cancer," says Aggarwal of the M.D. Anderson Cancer Center at the University of Texas.

Scientists are finding that curry powder, used in Indian cooking, has many healthful benefits.

The curcumin in curry seems to shut down genes that trigger the development and the spread of breast cancer, animal studies in Aggarwal's lab suggest. And a preliminary human study suggests curcumin supplements might be able to stabilize pancreatic cancer, he says.

Studies in humans also have linked frequent use of turmeric spice to lower rates of breast, prostate and colon cancer, he says.

Americans don't need to wait for the proof on curry to enjoy a diet that includes more of this spice, says Alamelu Vairavan, co-author of the book *Healthy South Indian Cooking*. "You don't need to gulp supplements," she says, adding that cooks can find turmeric in Indian specialty shops and in most grocery stores.

—Kathleen Fackelmann

CHAPTER SEVEN

LOOKING TO THE FUTURE

Ads for expensive magnetic-wave devices claim that they can relieve pain, improve blood flow, and improve the body's natural healing process when the magnets are applied to any area of the body. Magnetic field therapy is still very new. Many practitioners of conventional medicine do not recommend it.

All the same, research on magnetic therapy is ongoing. But whether magnets are effective treatment tools or not, they—and other alternative therapies—are becoming part of American culture. As consumer interest in complementary health care continues to mushroom, the demand will help to shape the course of medicine: its cost, availability, style, regulation, and variety of treatment options. And one of the most important factors in the future of

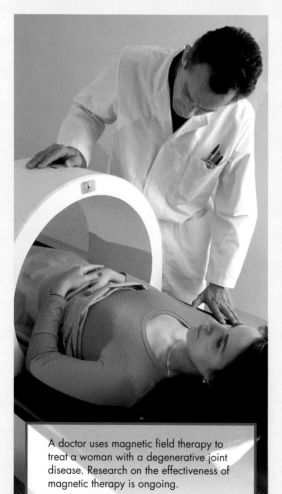

A doctor uses magnetic field therapy to treat a woman with a degenerative joint disease. Research on the effectiveness of magnetic therapy is ongoing.

What it costs

USA TODAY phoned 10 top hotel, destination and resort spas across the nation to find out the cost and length of a deep-tissue massage. Here is what we found[1]:

The spa	The massage	The cost	The length
The Spa at The Broadmoor **Colorado Springs**	Deep-tissue massage	$140	65 minutes
The Spa at The Homestead **Hot Springs, Va.**	Deep-tissue massage	$130	50 minutes
Spa Bellagio at The Bellagio **Las Vegas**	Combination massage	$120	50 minutes
The Waihua Spa at the Ritz-Carlton **Kapalua, Maui**	Deep-tissue massage	$130	60 minutes
The Peninsula Spa and Health Club **New York**	Deep-tissue massage	$150	60 minutes
The Spa at The Breakers **Palm Beach, Fla.**	Deep-tissue massage	$150	50 minutes
The Spa at the Four Seasons **Philadelphia**	Deep-tissue massage	$120	50 minutes
The Spa at Bacara Resort **Santa Barbara, Calif.**	Deep-tissue massage	$145	50 minutes
Willow Stream, The Spa at Fairmont **Scottsdale, Ariz.**	Sports massage	$135	60 minutes
Sea Island Spa at The Cloister **Sea Island, Ga.**	Therapeutic massage	$110	50 minutes

1 – Does not include taxes, service charges or gratuities.
Source: USA TODAY research

By Suzy Parker, USA TODAY, 2004

alternative medicine is whether health insurance companies will agree to cover the cost of therapies. For example, in the twenty-first century, many insurance companies are paying for treatments such as acupuncture and chiropractic therapy.

REGULATION

Some states already have set licensing standards for practitioners of alternative medicine. This helps more Americans understand the potential benefits and pitfalls of this type of care. But it also limits

News
SECTION A
NEWS.USATODAY.COM

July 31, 2009

From the Pages of USA TODAY

More trying alternative therapies
$34B spent per year on unconventional methods

Although Americans may complain about the high cost of health care, they're willing to shell out roughly $34 billion a year on alternative therapies that aren't covered by insurance, according to a survey released Thursday.

That's a growth of more than 25% in the past decade, says a survey of 23,000 American adults by the Centers for Disease Control and Prevention (CDC) and the National Institutes of Health (NIH).

Alternative therapies, which range from herbs to yoga classes, account for 11% of the total amount that Americans spend personally on all health care.

Americans don't always use these treatments under a doctor's guidance.

The bulk of these expenses, $22 billion, goes to "self-care," or treatments such as homeopathic medications and fish oil capsules that people buy without necessarily seeking a doctor's advice, the survey says.

Linda Lee, director of the Johns Hopkins Integrative Medicine & Digestive

who can practice alternative therapies and what standards of quality they must meet.

In addition, regulation of the practice of alternative medicine varies from state to state. This can lead to confusion among consumers, insurers, and medical providers. It may not be clear what therapies are safe and useful. As alternative medicine becomes more and more popular, government officials will come under new pressure from consumer groups and the medical profession to set new, consistent standards for training and quality of care.

Nowhere will the pressure be stronger than on the makers of herbal products. Many critics believe state and U.S. regulators should

Center near Baltimore [MD], says she's concerned about patients who "self-prescribe" alternative therapies, often without telling their doctors.

"An open dialogue with our patients only improves our ability to care for them," Lee says.

She points out that the high use of alternative therapies doesn't mean that these patients reject conventional medical treatment.

Many people combine conventional and complementary approaches, Lee says. For example, cancer patients may undergo chemotherapy at a hospital, but also use acupuncture for chronic pain.

The study shows that conventional doctors need to learn as much as possible about alternative therapies, Lee says, "not so they can necessarily prescribe or profit from them, but so they understand what it is their patients are hoping to gain and advise patients as to their appropriate use."

Annual out-of-pocket spending for alternative medicine among adults

- Natural products (such as the herb echinacea or fish oil): $14.8 billion
- Office visits: $11.9 billion
- Classes (such as yoga, tai chi): $4.1 billion
- Homeopathic medicine: $2.9 billion
- Relaxation techniques: $0.2 billion
- Total costs: $33.9 billion

Source: National Health Interview Survey, 2007, of 23,000 adults

The study's results also show the importance of rigorous scientific research into alternative therapies, says Josephine Briggs, director of the NIH's National Center for Complementary and Alternative Medicine.

—*Liz Szabo*

play a stronger role in regulating the huge supply of over-the-counter herbal and dietary supplements available to the public. But many regulators say they do not have the resources to do an effective job of overseeing this fast-growing field. And industries that make and market herbal remedies are not likely to back down in the face of efforts to regulate their products.

Questions with which consumers and experts are grappling include these:

- When is a natural substance, such as an herb, safe to consider as a medicine, and when is it a food? When should it be regulated by the government as a medicine? For example, caffeine is a natural substance that has physical effects. Should coffee, tea, and soft drinks with caffeine be treated as drugs?

- How effective are "functional foods," and how strictly should they be regulated? (Functional foods are products such as orange juice to which extra calcium has been added or tea to which ginger has been added to fight nausea. Consumers often want to buy functional foods because the labels on these foods claim health benefits.)

- When is a treatment real medicine, and when is it not? Is a technique such as massage or aromatherapy a medical procedure? How much training should people be required to have before they can perform acupuncture, prescribe herbs, or teach qigong?

Alternative treatments such as massage therapy are not counted as a medical procedure and are sometimes not covered by insurance. As alternative medicine becomes more popular in the United States, consumers will have to figure out how it fits into their budgets for medical care.

- And what about conventional Western medicine? It doesn't always work. Many treatments are experimental. Some prescription medications have dangerous side effects, just as alternative remedies sometimes do. Should Western and alternative treatments be held to the same scientific standards? Should alternative treatments be held to looser or to stricter standards than those for conventional therapies?

Should insurance companies treat all therapies—conventional and alternative—the same? Or should they set up different rules for conventional treatment and alternative ones?

As alternative medicine grows and matures, Americans will become more familiar with the huge range of alternative treatments. Policy makers, medical practitioners, and patients will have to consider all these questions very carefully.

The best approach is always to be a smart consumer of medical treatments. Do your research with a trusted adult, and talk to your family doctor before making any decisions. Ask questions and make sure you understand all the benefits and risks of any therapy before deciding on a treatment. After all, it is your health and safety that are most important.

GLOSSARY

acupressure: the stimulation of blocked energy points using finger or hand pressure instead of acupuncture needles

acupuncture: the insertion of thin needles at strategic points of the body to block pain or restore health. According to traditional Chinese thought, acupuncture stimulates or disperses energy, or chi, that flows along invisible channels in the body.

Alexander Technique: a system of verbal coaching and gentle hands-on corrections to improve posture, movement, and breathing. This technique was developed by an Australian actor—Frederick Matthias Alexander—in the early 1900s.

alternative medicine: a type of health care that relies on techniques and philosophies of health that are outside of the disease-based theories at the root of conventional Western medicine. Alternative techniques include many options, such as herbs, natural oils, massage, and spiritual methods to maintain health, relieve pain, and treat other symptoms. Alternative medicine does not rely on surgery, complex technology, or prescription drugs.

aromatherapy: a method of inhaling or applying to the skin essential oils from plants to relax or to heal physical or emotional disorders

Ayurvedic medicine: a holistic approach developed in India more than five thousand years ago that combines plant-based products, diet adjustments, exercise, massage, and meditation, among other techniques. The goal of Ayurveda is to maintain balance and harmony in the body as a way to promote good health. To do so, Ayurvedic medicine puts equal emphasis on the mind, the body, and the spirit.

biofeedback: a method of learning to control bodily functions such as heart rate, blood pressure, and skin temperature using feedback from electronic monitoring devices along with willpower and deep relaxation

chi: the body's vital energy, as defined in traditional Chinese medicine

chiropractic treatment: a method of correcting misalignments in the bones of the spinal column to relieve pressure on the nerves that are connected to various tissues and organs

complementary medicine: a range of alternative healing techniques (herbs, massage, acupuncture, etc.) that patients often use along with conventional medicine to relieve stress and pain and to recover from disease and injury. Complementary medicine is sometimes also called integrative medicine.

conventional medicine: a tradition of healing and treatment based on the idea that disease causes all illness. Medically trained doctors of conventional, or Western, medicine focus on diagnosing and treating the symptoms of people who are ill. They use synthetic medications, surgery, and technology to achieve these goals.

dietary supplement: a product that is meant to add to, not replace, a healthy diet. Examples include vitamins, minerals, herbs, amino acids, and other substances that are taken by mouth. Some supplements can be dangerous if taken in large doses or if they are not proven to be safe.

energy therapy: a system of healing that uses devices to measure the body's electromagnetic forces to detect imbalances that practitioners believe can be signs of illness

guided imagery: a psychological technique for fighting stress and illness through imagining positive outcomes to situations

herbal medicine: plant-based medicines made from leaves, stems, seeds, and other plant parts. They may be taken as teas, syrups, ointments, or in pill form. Herbal medications are used to treat a variety of conditions such as pain, sleeplessness, and inflammation. Herbal medicines can be dangerous and should not be taken with prescription drugs. Be sure to consult your doctor before taking any herbal medication.

holistic medicine: an approach to healing in which the body's various systems (mind, body, spirit) are treated as working together as parts of a whole

homeopathy: a system of medical treatment based on the idea that "like cures like." Patients take very small doses of a prescribed natural substance in diluted form to stimulate the body's natural defenses and cure the person of a particular disease.

hypnotherapy: a method of improving concentration, alertness, and relaxation using hypnosis. Hypnosis is a state of deep relaxation in which a patient becomes open to suggestion.

magnetic field therapy: a noninvasive treatment using magnets applied to specific areas of the body to treat broken bones, pain, and stress

massage: manipulation of soft tissues (muscles, skin, tendons, etc.) to relieve stress, muscle soreness, and pain

meditation: a mental state of awareness and peacefulness that may be achieved through quiet contemplation of an object, an idea, a phrase, or an image. The goal of meditation is to find spiritual peace as well as relief from physical stress.

music therapy: the use of music to treat psychological and physical illness and to reduce stress

naturopathy: a holistic approach to healing that includes natural remedies, such as herbs, massage, dietary changes, reflexology, acupuncture, talk therapy, and other options

osteopathy: a form of holistic (mind, body, spirit), hands-on medicine developed in the United States in the late 1800s. Osteopaths work with what they believe to be the body's ability to heal itself. In a typical session, an osteopath gently manipulates bones and joints to try to release trauma and stress. DOs (doctors of osteopathic medicine) are highly trained professionals who are licensed to practice osteopathic medicine and perform surgery.

qigong: a form of traditional Chinese medicine that combines physical and breathing exercises with meditation to maintain health and wellness

reflexology: a system of using finger pressure to stimulate nerve endings in the foot or hand to restore health to organs and body parts

Reiki: an energy-based therapy in which a therapist places his or her hands on or near the body to adjust the flow of energy from the therapist to the patient. Reiki can help with relaxation and stress relief. Reiki comes from the Japanese words *rei* (universal spirit) and *qi* (life force energy).

rolfing: a trademarked approach developed by Dr. Ida P. Rolf in the early 1900s to manipulate tissues and muscles to lessen lower back pain and to improve posture, flexibility, and general movement of the body; also called Rolfing Structural Integration, or Rolfing SI

tai chi: a set of ancient Chinese physical movements combined with deep breathing and meditation. Tai chi was developed as a martial art and is also practiced for health reasons to help reduce stress and increase flexibility.

therapeutic touch: a technique in which a therapist works to rebalance a patient's energy field to restore health. The therapist moves his or her hands a few inches above the patient's body to find breaks or blockages in the energy field. The therapist then touches key parts of the body to move energy to the patient to boost healing.

yoga: an ancient Hindu spiritual practice that includes stretching, breathing, and meditation techniques that can also create emotional and physical relaxation and well-toned muscles

RESOURCES

American Association of Naturopathic Physicians
4435 Wisconsin Avenue NW
Suite 403
Washington, DC 20016
866-538-2267
http://www.naturopathic.org
This website offers a wealth of information about naturopathic medicine, including what it is and how to find a naturopath in your area. Links to information about a range of health issues—from nutrition and weight to respiratory and heart ailments to mental health issues—are included, along with links where you can listen to naturopaths discussing a variety of medical topics.

American Chiropractic Association (ACA)
1701 Clarendon Boulevard
Arlington, VA 22209
703-276-8800
http://www.acatoday.org
Click the "Patients" tab at the top of the home page of this website to get information about how to find a chiropractor, for tips on chiropractic health and wellness, for more on the latest research, and to get answers to commonly asked questions about chiropractic therapy.

American Herbalists Guild
P.O. Box 230741
Boston, MA 02123
857-350-3128
http://americanherbalistsguild.com
This organization is geared toward practitioners of herbalism. Its website is a good first stop for finding an herbalist in your area.

American Music Therapy Association
8455 Colesville Road
Suite 1000
Silver Spring, MD 20910
301-589-3300
http://www.musictherapy.org
This website provides good information about music therapy and how to find a music therapist in your area. Links to more information about music therapy research, events, and trends are also available at the site.

American Osteopathic Association (AOA)
142 East Ontario Street
Chicago, IL 60611
800 621-1773
http://www.osteopathic.org/Pages/default.aspx
The website of the AOA is a good starting point to learn more about osteopathy, how to find an osteopath in your area, and what to expect in sessions with an osteopath.

Association for Applied Psychophysiology and Biofeedback, Inc.
10200 West 44th Avenue
Suite 304
Wheat Ridge, CO 80033
800-477-8892
http://www.aapb.org/consumers.html
This website is a great source of information about biofeedback. It offers information on treatments for a wide range of disorders; and on how to find a biofeedback provider. A glossary of terms, answers to frequently asked questions, and much more are included.

Center for Science in the Public Interest
1220 L Street NW
Suite 300
Washington, DC 20005
202-332-9110
http://www.cspinet.org
Go to this website for more information about food safety, food labeling, nutrition and health, and how to eat green.

National Center for Homeopathy
101 South Whiting Street
Suite 315
Alexandria, VA 22304
703-548-7790
http://homeopathic.org
This website is a good place to start to learn more about the definition of homeopathy, what its goals and treatment options are, and how to choose a reputable homeopath. The site also has a list of links to related organizations.

National Institutes of Health, National Center for Complementary and Alternative Medicine (NCCAM)
NCCAM Clearinghouse
P.O. Box 7923
Gaithersburg, MD 20898
888-644-6226
http://nccam.nih.gov
This website is an excellent resource for a wide variety of information about complementary and alternative medicine. You can learn more about how to be an informed CAM consumer and how to find a reputable CAM practitioner in your area. You can also get more information about many health topics and find links to videos and other multimedia to learn more about what is involved in different types of CAM therapy.

SOURCE NOTES

21 Mayo Clinic, *Mayo Clinic Book of Alternative Medicine* (New York: Time Inc. Home Entertainment, 2010), 19.

48 Bill Moyers, *Healing and the Mind* (New York: Knopf Doubleday, 1995), 226.

SELECTED BIBLIOGRAPHY

Augustyn Lawton, Sandra. *Complementary and Alternative Medicine Information for Teens*. Aston, PA: Omnigraphics, 2008.

Haugen, David M., ed. *Alternative Medicine*. Detroit: Greenhaven Press, 2009.

Mayo Clinic. *Mayo Clinic Book of Alternative Medicine*. New York: Time Inc. Home Entertainment, 2010.

Moyers, Bill. *Healing and the Mind*. New York: Knopf Doubleday, 1995.

National Center for Complementary and Alternative Medicine. http://nccam.nih.gov (August 2011).

Rolf Institute of Structural Integration. "What Is Rolfing® Structural Integration?" http://www.rolf.org/about (August 2011).

FURTHER READING AND WEBSITES

Books

Chryssicas, Mary Kaye. *Breathe: Yoga for Teens*. New York: DK Publishing, 2007.

Haugen, David M. *Alternative Medicine*. Opposing Viewpoints series. Farmington Hills, MI: Greenhaven Press, 2008.

Hyde, Margaret O., and Elizabeth H. Forsyth. *Stress 101: An Overview for Teens*. Minneapolis: Twenty-First Century Books, 2008.

Langwith, Jacqueline. *Alternative Medicine*. Introducing Issues with Opposing Viewpoints series. Farmington Hills, MI: Greehnaven Press, 2009.

Mayo Clinic. *Alternative Medicine and Your Health: Compact Guide to Fitness and Health*. Rochester, MN: 2004.

Miller, Debra A. *Alternative Therapies*. Current Controversies series. Farmington Hills, MI: Greenhaven Press, 2008.

Strelecky, David. *Complementary and Alternative Health Care*. Ferguson's Careers in Focus series. New York: Ferguson Publishing Co., 2009.

Wallerstein, Claire. *Alternative Medicine*. Need to Know series. Portsmouth, NH: Heinemann, 2005.

Websites

Mayo Clinic
http://www.mayoclinic.com/health/alternative-medicine/PN00001

This link from the internationally renowned Mayo Clinic offers an excellent introduction to complementary and alternative medicine (CAM). It includes additional links to a wide range of related information to help readers understand CAM options and to make informed decisions about CAM care.

Quackwatch
http://www.quackwatch.org

Quackwatch is a broad network of people concerned about fraud, fads, and myths in the field of health and medicine. The website offers a wide range of links to information to help readers identify and avoid fraud in treatments for physical diseases and emotional disorders, medical devices, drugs, and various alternative therapies. The site provides information on how to spot false advertising and also offers guidance on healthy living.

United States Department of Agriculture, ChooseMyPlate.gov
USDA Center for Nutrition Policy and Promotion
http://www.choosemyplate.gov

Visit this website to learn more about MyPlate—the USDA's food guidance system. You'll find helpful information about basic food groups, healthy eating habits, weight-loss information, and print and interactive tools for more information in English and in Spanish, including personalized food planning and daily exercise programs.

Expand learning beyond the printed book. Download free, complementary educational resources for this book from our website, www.lerneresource.com

INDEX

ABOUT THE AUTHOR

Catherine G. Davis is a writer and editor of books for young people. She makes her home in Minneapolis, Minnesota.

PHOTO ACKNOWLEDGMENTS

The images in this book are used with the permission of: © Gyro Photography/ amanaimagesRF/Getty Images, pp. 1, 3; © Adam Gault/SPL/Science Photo Library/ Getty Images, p. 5; © Robert Deutsch/USA TODAY, pp. 7, 19; © Tetra Images/ Getty Images, p. 10; © Bruno Vincent/Getty Images, p. 12; © Dan MacMedan/USA TODAY, p. 13; © Larry Armstrong, Freelance/USA TODAY, p. 20; © John Sommers II, Freelance/USA TODAY, p. 29; © iStockphoto.com/Vesna Sajn, p. 31; © marilyn barbone/Shutterstock.com, p. 38; © Will & Deni McIntyre/Photo Researchers, Inc., p. 43; © iStockphoto.com/Paula Connelly, p. 53; © Olivier Voisin/Photo Researchers, Inc., p. 57; AP Photo/Dave Martin, p. 59; © Air Rabbit/Digital Vision/Getty Images, p. 61; © Ira Weiny/Alamy, p. 65; © Steven Errico/Digital Vision/Getty Images, p. 69; © Eileen Blass/USA TODAY, p. 75; © Jaime Kowal/Workbook Stock/Getty Images, p. 80; © USA TODAY, p. 81; © Andy Crawford/Dorling Kindersley/Getty Images, p. 89; © Dennis Cox/Alamy, p. 92; © FotoosVanRobin/Flickr/Getty Images, p. 95; © Veronique Burger/Photo Researchers, Inc., p. 96; © Anne Ryan/USA TODAY, p. 100.

Front cover: © Gyro Photography/amanaimagesRF/Getty Images.

Main body text set in USA TODAY Roman 10/15.